100

THINGS TO DO IN

CONNECTICUT

BEFORE YOU

DIE

T0275005

Lighthouse Point Park in New Haven,
courtesy of the Connecticut Office of Tourism

100

THINGS TO DO IN
CONNECTICUT
BEFORE YOU
DIE

• •

ANASTASIA MILLS HEALY

Library of Congress Control Number: 2023951756

ISBN: 9781681065144

Design by Jill Halpin

Printed in the United States of America
24 25 26 27 28   5 4 3 2

We (the publisher and the author) have done our best to provide the most accurate information available when this book was completed. However, we make no warranty, guarantee, or promise about the accuracy, completeness, or currency of the information provided, and we expressly disclaim all warranties, express or implied. Please note that attractions, company names, addresses, websites, and phone numbers are subject to change or closure, and this is outside of our control. We are not responsible for any loss, damage, injury, or inconvenience that may occur due to the use of this book. When exploring new destinations, please do your homework before you go. You are responsible for your own safety and health when using this book.

DEDICATION

For everyone sitting at the kitchen table on a Saturday morning wondering what to do.

GRISWOLD INN
SINCE 1776
ESSEX • CONNECTICUT

CONTENTS

• •

Music and Entertainment

Sports and Recreation

• •

• •

Shopping and Fashion

• •

Greenwich Avenue,
courtesy of Anastasia Mills Healy

Gillette Castle,
courtesy of Anastasia Mills Healy

PREFACE

The options for things to do in Connecticut are endless, so picking 100 total in five categories was challenging. My goal was to showcase the state's variety of experiences and to highlight special, uniquely Connecticut places.

I will include some wonderful places that didn't make it into this book in my monthly Connecticut tourism-focused email. I am always learning, and I'd love to hear about any of your favorite spots that I've missed. Look for the Google form on my website stashamillshealy.com.

Argia Mystic, courtesy of the
Connecticut Office of Tourism

ACKNOWLEDGMENTS

I am grateful to everyone who recommended beloved locations to be included in this book and to the Connecticut Office of Tourism for providing many of the photos.

Lobster roll, courtesy of Anastasia Mills Healy

FOOD
AND DRINK

TRY A CLAM PIE
AT FRANK PEPE'S

Many people would make a pained face at the suggestion of clams on a pizza. But since Connecticut has hundreds of miles of shoreline, clams are not a surprising topping. Frank Pepe Pizzeria Napoletana made the original "apizza" in 1925, and this New Haven restaurant has been serving this crispier Neapolitan-style pizza ever since. The white clam pie has no tomato sauce or mozzarella, just clams, loads of garlic, pecorino Romano, olive oil, and oregano. Add bacon for an extra layer of flavor and leave room for dessert as there are Italian bakeries in walking distance. Other Frank Pepe locations have opened, but the first—with its seasoned ovens and history—stands out. Pepe's of course has more traditional pies for the mollusk shy.

157 Wooster St., New Haven, 203-865-5762
order.pepespizzeria.com/store/frank-pepes-new-haven

OTHER FAMOUS NEW HAVEN PIZZA SPOTS

Sally's Apizza
237 Wooster St., New Haven, 203-624-5271
sallysapizza.com

Modern Apizza
874 State St., New Haven, 203-776-5306
modernapizza.com

DIG INTO A WARM, CONNECTICUT-STYLE LOBSTER ROLL
AT ABBOTT'S

Forget about the cold, mayonnaise-entrenched Maine lobster salad sandwich because the warm, buttered, Connecticut-style lobster roll is the way to go since it was invented here. First served in Milford in the 1920s, a lobster roll should star big chunks of fresh lobster meat that are shiny with, but not overpowered by, melted butter. Spooned into a toothsome, toasted, buttered roll and served with a bag of potato chips and coleslaw, it's an ideal summer lunch—preferably eaten barefoot at the waterfront. As with pizza and ice cream, there's fierce competition over the state's best lobster roll. The tiny village of Noank is a good place to begin as the location of the longer-standing Abbott's Lobster in the Rough (founded in 1947). Order inside, take a seat on a picnic bench overlooking the Mystic River, crack open your BYOB beer, and dig into a Connecticut shoreline classic.

Abbott's
117 Pearl St., Noank, 860-536-7719
abbottslobster.com

DISCOVER STEW LEONARD'S
HANDCRAFTED ICE CREAM

Connecticut is home to a healthy number of dairy farms, and all this fresh cream and milk in the hands of artisan ice cream makers has resulted in a crowded field of outstanding purveyors, but Stew Leonard's soft serve vanilla and old-fashioned vanilla are exceptional. Relatively unknown outside of the tristate area, Stew's operates the world's largest dairy store (per *Ripley's Believe It or Not!*) and also sells its products in its own destination-worthy grocery stores. In addition to amazing dairy products, Stew's quality is hard to beat on all fronts, from produce to meat and homemade soups. Animatronic characters are placed throughout the Norwalk headquarters store to entertain kids. Don't even try to resist the ice cream counter you pass on the way out. Bonus: if you spend $200, an ice cream is free.

100 Westport Ave., Norwalk, 203-847-7214
stewleonards.com/locations/stew-leonards-of-norwalk

TASTE TEST OTHER GREAT CONNECTICUT ICE CREAM

Arethusa Farm Dairy
822 Bantam Rd., Bantam, 860-361-6460
1020 Chapel St., New Haven, 203-390-5114
975 Farmington Ave., West Hartford, 860-726-4593
arethusafarm.com

Ferris Acres Creamery
144 Sugar St., Newtown, 203-426-8803
ferrisacrescreamery.com

Mystic Drawbridge Ice Cream
2 W Main St., Mystic, 860-572-7978
mysticdrawbridgeicecream.com

Rich Farm
691 Oxford Rd., Oxford, 203-881-1040
409 Hill St., Bristol, 860-261-4486
7 Station Rd. D1, Brookfield, 475-289-2316
richfarmicecream.com

STEP BACK IN TIME
AT THE GRISWOLD INN

One of the longest continually operating inns in the US, the Griswold Inn in the charming seaport village of Essex first opened its doors in 1776. Step inside and soak up the unique atmosphere of rooms adorned with collectible books and outstanding maritime art. Belly up to the bar in the tavern that is packed with memorabilia; sample a wine flight and cheese board in the wine bar; or have a bite in the library or gun room where historic firearms, some locally made, ornament the walls. The cuisine highlights classic New England fare such as a creamy clam chowder and perfectly roasted cod, and there's a kids' menu for the younger set. Don't miss the inn's own flavorful Revolutionary Ale.

36 Main St., Essex, 860-767-1776
griswoldinn.com

TIP
Ask for literature about the Griswold Inn's history at the front desk.

SHOW SOME SPIRIT
AT THE LITCHFIELD DISTILLERY

Like farm-to-table dining, seed-to-glass distilling uses ingredients from local farms to produce outstanding results. From the Baker family behind Crystal Rock Water comes Litchfield Distillery, which sources grains and fruit from around their western Connecticut base for their award-winning bourbon, vodka, gin, and agave spirits. You might question flavors like blueberry vodka and coffee bourbon, but don't knock 'em until you've tried 'em! Tastings follow the tour. They sell premixed cocktails in glass bottles containing quaffs like old-fashioneds and cosmopolitans. Other product extensions include cans of spiked lemonade; the Litchfielder (bourbon, maple syrup, and lemon juice), and a Batcherita—a margarita-inspired mix of agave spirits and lime juice with a touch of orange flavor. Although you can't call it tequila if it's not made in Mexico, Litchfield Distillery imports agave nectar from Mexico, distills it in their facility, and ages it in pre-used bourbon barrels. Bottoms up!

569 Bantam Rd., Litchfield, 860-361-6503
litchfielddistillery.com

TAP INTO CONNECTICUT'S BREWERY SCENE
AT ELICIT BREWING

There are more than 125 craft breweries in Connecticut that run the gamut from waterside hot spots and farm-based settings to closet-size passion projects. Of special note is Manchester's Elicit Brewing Company & Beer Garden, which curates brews from around the state (and beyond) in addition to serving its own. If you don't have the time or inclination to spend days giving your Untappd app a workout, this is a one-stop shop for an expertly selected overview of the state's suds. Located outside Hartford, Elicit has dozens of taps, a beer hall, a full bar, and an arcade.

165 Adams St., Manchester, 860-791-8440
elicitbrewing.com

TIP
Find a brewery near you or create your own beer itinerary at ctbeer.com.

RAISE A PINT AT THESE STANDOUT BREWERIES, TOO

Charter Oak Brewing Co. and Taproom
39B Shelter Rock Rd., Danbury, 203-616-5268
charteroakbrewing.com

Fox Farm Brewery
62 Music Vale Rd., Salem
foxfarmbeer.com

Stony Creek Brewery
5 Indian Neck Ave., Branford, 203-433-4545
stonycreekbeer.com

Two Roads Brewing Company
1700 Stratford Ave., Stratford, 203-335-2010
tworoadsbrewing.com

SUCK DOWN SOME OYSTERS
AT SHELL & BONES OYSTER BAR AND GRILL

Among restaurants throughout the state that have an oyster focus, New Haven's Shell & Bones stands out. First, you've got to love the name, a takeoff on Yale's infamous Skull and Bones secret society. There's no secret here, though, about why this waterfront City Point restaurant is always packed. Fresh and sustainable is the operating mantra applied to not only seafood but to the soups, stocks, sauces, and desserts made daily in-house. As good for a business lunch as for a romantic dinner, Shell & Bones has an outdoor heated and covered deck, and a fireplace sets the sleek indoors aglow when the frost sets in. If you don't have an expense account, stop in for happy hour Monday through Friday from 3 to 5 p.m. for half-price oysters and $6 cocktails and wine.

100 S Water St., New Haven, 203-787-3466
shellandbones.com

TIP

If you want oysters that are guaranteed to be locally sourced, buy directly from the fishermen at Mystic Oysters. They're sustainably farmed year-round and sold at a no-frills storefront on Schooner Wharf where a limited menu also includes hot and cold lobster rolls and clam chowder.

15 Holmes St., Mystic, 860-333-7961
mysticoysters.com

SAVOR EVERY BITE
AT THE RESTAURANT AT WINVIAN

With a menu that changes daily, The Restaurant at Winvian Farm expertly prepares creative three-course dinners such as a crudo of kampachi starter and hand-rolled ravioli filled with guinea hen and chestnut as a pasta course, followed by a duo of braised short rib and New York strip steak. The restaurant practices seed-to-table dining with ingredients sourced from the on-property organic gardens, greenhouses, apiary, and henhouse. A series of charming dining rooms with fireplaces are decorated with antiques, oil paintings, and Oriental rugs, enveloping diners in the warmth of a 1775 farmhouse. Accompanying wines are definitely not an afterthought, with an enviable cellar and knowledgeable servers. The AAA Five Diamond restaurant is part of a unique Relais & Châteaux hotel with 18 themed cottages: the $125 per person prix fixe is a bargain compared to the $800-and-up bill for an overnight.

155 Alain White Rd., Morris, 860-567-9600
winvian.com

EXPERIENCE A NEW ENGLAND CLAMBAKE
ON SHEFFIELD ISLAND

A New England tradition, a clambake traditionally includes clams, corn on the cob, potatoes, salad, and dessert. It's even better when you don't have to cook it yourself. Add a boat ride and a lighthouse and you've hit the New England summer trifecta. A cruise offered by the Norwalk Seaport Association navigates among a chain of islands off Norwalk and includes the opportunity to explore the 52-acre Sheffield Island with its beautiful lighthouse and to enjoy a clambake under the stars. Held on Tuesdays in summer (dates vary), the outing includes a ferry ticket, a tour of the 1868 lighthouse, and a clambake served in a tented pavilion on the lighthouse lawn. Bring your own beverages as well as bug spray to ward off twilight mosquitoes.

4 N Water St., Norwalk, 203-838-9444
seaport.org/clambakes

DINE AT A NEW HAVEN LEGEND,
THE UNION LEAGUE CAFE

You know you're in good hands with a fourth-generation French chef commanding the kitchen. Set in a Beaux Arts landmark building adjacent to the Shops at Yale and surrounded by downtown New Haven's theater and arts attractions, Union League Cafe is inspired by classic Parisian brasseries. With white tablecloths, coffered ceiling, and a formally attired waitstaff, the restaurant aims to re-create Old World charm. Come hungry for the six-course tasting menu or order à la carte, perhaps starting with grilled octopus accompanied by faro and beet hummus, and then digging into a perfectly cooked steak au poivre in a green peppercorn sauce. Restaurants taking the time to make soufflés are rare these days so place your order for the soufflé du jour when you order your entrée.

1032 Chapel St., New Haven, 203-562-4299
unionleaguecafe.com

TASTE THE FRESHNESS
AT ARETHUSA AL TAVOLO

It makes perfect sense that the team behind the outstanding products and exacting methods of Arethusa Farm Dairy would open a restaurant. Of course, you would think that the dairy products would be memorable but so are the high-quality, often regionally sourced produce, meat, and seafood. The relaxed location in quiet Bantam was once the village's general store. Begin with zucchini flowers stuffed with Arethusa's ricotta or the house-made Sepe Farm lamb merguez sausage followed by the popular, crisp, roasted duck breast glazed with Litchfield-sourced maple syrup. To finish, order the Arethusa cheese plate or stretch your legs and go next door to their dairy store for an ice cream cone (and a pint to go).

828 Bantam Rd., Bantam, 860-567-0043
arethusaaltavolo.com

SAMPLE CONNECTICUT-MADE WINE
AT AQUILA'S NEST

Yes, Connecticut makes wine and has a wine trail to prove it! There are 22 wineries and vineyards throughout the state producing everything from Riesling to brandy. Those who are really committed can use GPS to virtually stamp their in-app Connecticut Wine Passports. A front-runner is Aquila's Nest Vineyards, new on the scene in 2020 . . . just in time for the pandemic. Battling the odds with exceptional wine, a stunning location, a passionate spirit of community, and a packed calendar of events, Aquila's Nest is flourishing. Set on a hilltop overlooking 41 acres, the comfortable tasting room has various seating areas, a wine bar, and a baby grand piano. Outdoor spaces—including picnic tables, a pergola, and a gazebo—are lively in good weather; when a chill is in the air, firepits add to the ambiance. Try the flights to sample robust reds, dry whites, and even wine slushies.

56 Pole Bridge Rd., Newton, 203-518-4352
aquilasnestvineyards.com

FIND OUT WHAT THE FUSS IS ABOUT
AT PORT OF CALL

With a bar voted one of the best in America by *Esquire* and a chef nominated for a James Beard Award, Mystic's Port of Call is worthy of your attention. Tastefully decorated with not just inspiration but actual artifacts from Mystic's seafaring past, Port of Call is just off the main drag downtown, next to its sister restaurant Oyster Club where Renée Touponce is also executive chef. Opened in 2022, the small and elegant Port of Call feels like a custom-built yacht with a bar and floorboards crafted from historic ships. Flickering lamps, mirrored portholes, and tufted leather chairs add to the vibe. House specialty cocktails incorporate unusual ingredients like tonka beans and rice koji, and food offerings like pinchos, bacalaitos, and empanadas are the chef's takes on dishes she remembers fondly from her childhood. Using techniques like fermenting, curing, and preserving, her kitchens take their time with each dish.

15 Water St., Mystic, 860-980-3648
theportofcallct.com

PICK YOUR OWN PRODUCE
AT LYMAN ORCHARDS

There's nothing like the sweet taste of a perfectly ripe strawberry just plucked from the vine. With so many farms in Connecticut, there is no shortage of options for places to pick your own produce—and if there's a clinker in the box, you'll have no one to blame but yourself. Growing everything from pumpkins and Christmas trees to sunflowers and apples, farms invite visitors to pay for a container and fill it with their in-season produce. What you get: farm-fresh, healthy, organic food; a feeling of accomplishment; connection to the land so many of us are missing; and the knowledge that you're supporting critical local businesses. A farm with an impressive variety of produce is Lyman Orchards in Middlefield. Family run for hundreds of years, it offers pick-your-own apples, strawberries, raspberries, blueberries, peaches, pears, and nectarines as well as two under-the-radar berries—jostaberries and honeyberries. Stop by the store for other produce and goods like pies and jams made from their fruit.

105 South St., Middlefield, 860-349-6015
lymanorchards.com

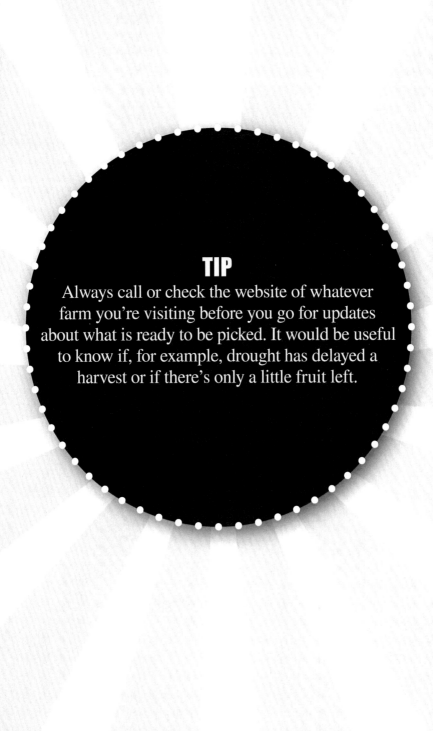

TIP

Always call or check the website of whatever farm you're visiting before you go for updates about what is ready to be picked. It would be useful to know if, for example, drought has delayed a harvest or if there's only a little fruit left.

ENJOY A MEAL
AT STONE ACRES FARM

Imagine driving up to a field and walking past haystacks to sit under fairy lights. Your table has fresh-cut flowers, and course after course of an exquisite dinner—sourced at least in part by the products of the earth under your feet—delight the senses. Some Connecticut farms occasionally schedule such events in collaboration with chefs, and others involve guests not only to eat but to also learn about farming, pick produce, and prepare meals. A working farm since 1765, Stone Acres Farm holds food-inspired events like cooking classes and educational workshops on its 63 acres throughout the year. Mystic's Oyster Club and Port of Call prepare their lauded dishes with this farm's produce, and their celebrated chef, Renée Touponce, has created memorable, sold-out dinners at Stone Acres that result in standing ovations.

393 N Main St., Stonington, 860-245-5127
stoneacresfarm.com

YOU CAN ALSO RESERVE A FARM DINNER AT ...

Hunts Brook Farm
108 Hunts Brook Rd., Quaker Hill, 860-912-2352
huntsbrookfarmct.com

Husky Meadows Farm
26 Doolittle Dr., Norfolk, 860-540-4757
huskymeadowsfarm.com

Rosedale Farms & Vineyards
25 E Weatogue St., Simsbury, 860-651-3926
rosedale1920.com

BITE INTO HISTORY
AT LOUIS' LUNCH

Louis' Lunch is a New Haven institution whose claim to fame is having made one of the world's first known hamburger sandwiches in 1900. It's a small, casual spot that still uses unique gas-powered vertical broilers manufactured in 1898. This method cooks the patties—a secret mix of five meats, hand-rolled and cooked to order—on both sides in probably some of the planet's most seasoned cast iron, and the fat drippings result in juicier burgers. There are rules here: the first is that there is no ketchup available or allowed; acceptable embellishments are cheese, tomato, and onion. Another rule is that the burgers are served on toasted white Pepperidge Farm bread, not buns. These traditions don't thrill everyone but they must be doing something right to be in business more than a century.

261 Crown St., New Haven, 203-562-5507
louislunch.com

TIP

Another Connecticut burger institution, Manchester's Shady Glen is a 1950s-style diner known for hand-mixed sodas, outstanding ice cream, and the Bernice Original Cheeseburger. Four slices of cheese extend from the round edge of the patty and are fried crisp to be nibbled from the edges or folded up under the top of the roll.

840 Middle Tpke. E, Manchester, 860-649-4245

TASTE THE WORLD'S BEST LOBSTER BENEDICT
AT KITCHEN LITTLE

It's challenging to find a sit-down restaurant that doesn't break the bank, but in the tourist mecca of Mystic, no less, this unicorn of a restaurant exists. However, it only serves breakfast, doesn't take reservations, and often has a line of people waiting to get in. Kitchen Little started welcoming customers in 1980, and this cozy spot is open daily (except Tuesdays) until 1 p.m. The best lobster (eggs) Benedict in the universe is made in this small, unassuming restaurant. Located in a residential area on the second floor of the Mystic Marina, it's a five-minute drive from the bustle of downtown. The extensive menu features egg dishes that reflect the seafaring and Portuguese heritages of the area like an asparagus and crab omelet and scrambled eggs with chorizo, jalapeños, and a Portuguese muffin. Those more inclined to the carb side of the menu will enter into a sugar coma after finishing the Cinna-Bun French Toast with cream cheese drizzle. No matter what you choose, it will be great: this little spot has been featured in national media like the Food Network and *Gourmet* magazine.

36 Quarry Rd., Mystic, 860-536-2122
kitchenlittle.org

LINGER AT
A BUFFET BRUNCH
AT THE WATER'S EDGE

Brunch buffets were disappearing before COVID, and subsequent health protocols wiped out many of them in all corners of the world. But brunch lovers, rejoice! You no longer have to choose sweet or savory, breakfast or lunch, waffles or smoked salmon—you can have it all. As its name suggests, Water's Edge Resort and Spa overlooks the Long Island Sound in Westbrook, midcoast. A sprawling complex with four restaurants, a beach, pool, and spa, the resort serves a lavish buffet brunch on Sundays from 9 a.m. to 3 p.m. Graze the fruit and salad bars and dig into a Nutella crepe, cheese blintz, or charcuterie spread. Pick your fillings for an omelet made to order. Look for the raw bar by the ice sculpture and then move on to the carving station. Entrées change weekly but one staple is the oven-roasted prime rib with thyme jus and horseradish. Don't pass up spectacular sides like three-cheese scalloped potatoes. Oh, and the desserts—cakes, tortes, French mini-pastries, and a cookie bar—are the icing on the um, well, you know what.

1525 Boston Post Rd., Westbrook, 860-577-3511
watersedgeresortandspa.com

INDULGE IN
HEAVENLY CHOCOLATE
AT BRIDGEWATER

Connecticut has a long history of producing fine chocolate starting when Christopher Leffingwell of Norwich opened the state's first chocolate mill in 1770. Today the state boasts numerous excellent artisan chocolatiers and even has a Chocolate Trail. With retail outlets in locations including Brookfield, Westport, and West Hartford, Bridgewater Chocolate is an elevated chocolate purveyor that gets it right. They use only the highest-quality ingredients and provide free samples without judgment. Their gift curation service saves time and bandwidth, and exquisite packaging conveys luxury item status. Big sellers are peanut butter patties, turtles, and toffee. A personal favorite is anything with marzipan filling, which is fresh, moist, and flavorful.

559 Federal Rd., Brookfield, 203-775-2286
bridgewaterchocolate.com

YOU CAN ALSO GET YOUR CHOCOLATE FIX AT THESE PLACES

BE Chocolat
Greenfield Hill Commons
75 Hillside Rd., Fairfield, 203-292-5981
bechocolat.com

Fascia's Chocolates
44 Chase River Rd., Waterbury, 203-753-0515
faschoc.com

Thorncrest Farm, LLC & Milk House Chocolates
280 Town Hill Rd., Goshen, 860-309-2545
milkhousechocolates.net

MOMIX Litchfield,
courtesy of the Connecticut Office of Tourism

MUSIC
AND ENTERTAINMENT

SEE A MUSICAL
AT THE GOODSPEED OPERA HOUSE

Overlooking the Connecticut River, the Goodspeed Opera House is one of the state's most recognizable buildings. Opened in 1877 to attract top talent and patrons traveling via steamboat from New York City, today Goodspeed continues to deliver on its mission to produce high-quality musicals in a one-of-a-kind setting. Yes, musicals—there has never been an opera production here. Three of the world's most famous musicals made their debuts at the Goodspeed: *Annie, Man of La Mancha*, and *Shenandoah*. In fact, 21 shows have made it to Broadway, and the theater has two special Tony Awards to attest to its standing as the Home of the American Musical: one for outstanding contributions to the American musical genre and the other for distinguished achievement for a regional theater. The theater has launched not only shows but stars including Ariana Grande and Idina Menzel.

6 Main St., East Haddam, 860-873-8668
goodspeed.org

TIP

Right next door, Gelston House Restaurant and Inn offers a prix fixe dinner for theatergoers as well as a late-night menu and several guest rooms.
8 Main St., East Haddam, 860-873-1411
gelstonhouse.com

CATCH THE NEXT BRUCE SPRINGSTEEN
AT TOAD'S PLACE

A who's who of rock royalty has stepped under the lights at Toad's Place, a legendary New Haven music venue. From the Rolling Stones and U2 to Cardi B. and Post Malone, Toad's Place books acts from diverse musical genres—on any given night, you might catch a reggae show, a techno DJ, or a night of blues. Some performers never attract bigger audiences than those in this 1,000-person-capacity club but others go on to pack arenas around the globe. Opened in 1975, Toad's can be mentioned in the same breath as other New Haven icons like Frank Pepe's and Louis' Lunch, which have weathered fads, economic vagaries, and vast changes in the business landscape. A documentary is in the works, and a book, *The Legendary Toad's Place: Stories from New Haven's Famed Music Venue*, takes readers behind the scenes.

300 York St., New Haven, 203-624-8623
toadsplace.com

SPEND A DAY
AT A COUNTY FAIR IN DURHAM

As far as entertainment goes, it's hard to beat a county fair. There are musical performances throughout the day plus carnival rides and games, oxen and horse pulls, demolition derbies, and monster truck shows. See your neighbors shine in a talent or joke contest or pick up a mic yourself for a karaoke ballad. Sample local beer, wine, and spirits and stuff yourself silly on corn dogs, kettle corn, and ice cream. Admire the goats, sheep, and cows competing for best in show. Learn how to make corn relish. Play cow plop bingo (if the cow poops on your number, you win). Say "awww!" continuously for a half hour as animals parade by in costumes. Marvel at the skills possessed by those making wood and metal sculptures in front of your eyes. Watch a magic show, pick a balloon animal, or go on a scavenger hunt. Observe weaving and milking demonstrations, and fireworks to top it all off. There are fairs throughout the state but Durham's has been happening every year for more than a century and attracts 200,000 people, so you know they've got this down.

24 Townhouse Rd., Durham, 860-349-9495
durhamfair.com

SING ALONG TO A FAVORITE BAND
AT SOUND ON SOUND MUSIC FESTIVAL

Connecticut's largest musical festival, Sound on Sound, draws 60,000 people to Bridgeport's Seaside Park over two days. Dave Matthews, Red Hot Chili Peppers, and Fairfield's own John Mayer are among the famous acts who have taken the stage. About 10 bands a day play on the same stage, one after the other from noon until 11 p.m. Once you stake the claim to your space, you can get comfortable, and you won't have to decide which bands to see as you do at other festivals when there are multiple stages with acts playing simultaneously. If you have to sit through bands you may not be too excited about, diversions include a Ferris wheel on-site, lots of food and drink vendors, and an entire waterfront park designed by Connecticut native Frederick Law Olmsted (of Central Park fame) to explore. If you're flush enough to consider tickets beyond general admission, there are options for VIP areas.

1 Barnum Dyke, Bridgeport
soundonsoundct.com

TAKE A LEAP OF FAITH
WITH LONG WHARF THEATRE

First presenting plays in 1965, the Tony Award–winning Long Wharf Theatre has been selling out performances in a Sargent Drive theater in New Haven for decades. Now, in response to COVID and the financial burden of a building, productions are no longer tethered to that theater in the interest of better community engagement. What that means is that Long Wharf Theatre productions are being staged in other area theaters, libraries, and even in private homes. How wonderful, innovative, and intimate to invite a handful of people into a living room to watch the masterful Kathleen Chalfant portray Joan Didion's grief in a staging of *The Year of Magical Thinking*. In addition to staging nationally recognized works, they also incubate local talent to provide a platform that brings more stories to light.

Various, 203-693-1486
longwharf.org

RETHINK YOUR IDEAS ABOUT DANCE
AT A PILOBOLUS PERFORMANCE

Two pioneering Washington, Connecticut–based dance companies have taken their exciting forms of contemporary dance to the world. The extremely athletic and flexible dancers in Pilobolus move together in ways that the average human wouldn't imagine possible. Formed in 1971, they've performed at the Olympic Games, the Oscars, and on Broadway. In summer, look locally for free, short performances in parks and other outdoor spaces. Otherwise, you can catch the Pilobolus troupe throughout the state, the country, and the world. A decade into its life, a Pilobolus cofounder started his own company, MOMIX. More theatrical than Pilobolus, MOMIX is masterful at combining dance with gymnastics and using props, lighting, and costumes to create stunning productions that have wowed audiences on five continents.

Pilobolus
860-868-0538
pilobolus.org

MOMIX
860-868-7454
momix.com

BE COOL
AT WESTPORT'S VERSOFEST

Connecticut's libraries are incredible resources for any number of reasons, from teaching skills to tracking down obscure information and showing movies. Westport's offerings are particularly robust as evidenced by its Verso Studios and annual VersoFest. Their state-of-the-art recording studio is at the ready for bands, music producers, podcasters, and authors creating audiobooks. The library's annual spring music and media conference and festival offers panels, workshops, exhibitions, and concerts that are cooler than anyone might expect library programming to be. Hear musician Chris Frantz (Talking Heads, Tom Tom Club) interview producer Steve Lillywhite (U2, the Rolling Stones); take a rock photography master class; watch the Smithereens; see an exhibition of Alice Cooper's costumes and props; listen to a discussion about cutting-edge female/androgynous rock fashion; or learn about Richard Butler's (the Psychedelic Furs) visual arts endeavors. Who knew there were so many hipsters in Fairfield County?

20 Jesup Rd., Westport, 203-291-4828
westportlibrary.org/services/verso-studios

DREAM OF SUGAR PLUM FAIRIES
AT *THE NUTCRACKER*

Who can resist the sword-fighting mice, human-size nutcracker, and towering Christmas tree of a *Nutcracker Suite* performance? Many families dress up and take in the magic of this dreamy Balanchine ballet to help get in the holiday spirit. The Connecticut Ballet has performed this classic hundreds of times since 1984 but the energy of the children in the production and the palpable joy of the audience keep it fresh. Both Stamford's Palace Theatre and Hartford's Bushnell Center schedule December performances featuring guest stars from the American Ballet Theatre and New York City Ballet. Check listings to see if dancers will be signing autographs and taking pictures, which make the day even more special for aspiring young dancers.

Bushnell Center for the Performing Arts
166 Capitol Ave., Hartford, 860-987-5900
bushnell.org

Palace Theatre
61 Atlantic St., Stamford, 203-325-4466
palacestamford.org

Connecticut Ballet
860-293-1039
connecticutballet.org

GET JAZZY
AT THE LITCHFIELD JAZZ FESTIVAL

You don't need to go to New Orleans for great jazz. The Litchfield Jazz Festival started off with a bang in 1996 with Diana Krall and Terence Blanchard in the lineup, and the festival is going stronger than ever today. After years at the Goshen Fairgrounds, the festival now takes place in the new, acoustically excellent, and air-conditioned 415-seat Tisch Family Auditorium on the campus of the Frederick Gunn School, with unobstructed views from every seat.

Tisch Family Auditorium Thomas S. Perakos Arts and Community Center
at the Frederick Gunn School
22 Kirby Rd., Washington, 860-567-4162
litchfieldjazzfest.com

OTHER JAZZ VENUES

Jazz lovers in the Hartford area descend on the Performance Pavilion in Bushnell Park for the **Greater Hartford Festival of Jazz**, New England's largest free public jazz festival. Chuck Mangione, the Duke Ellington Orchestra, and Arturo Sandoval are among the many who have performed at this festival since it began in 1991.
Bushnell Park, 1 Jewell St., Hartford, 860-490-2199
hartfordjazz.org

If an intimate jazz club in a small inn is more your style, head to the **Side Door Jazz Club** in the Old Lyme Inn. Voted one of the world's best jazz clubs by *DownBeat*, it's a casually sophisticated spot open on Fridays and Saturdays.
85 Lyme St., Old Lyme, 860-434-2600
thesidedoorjazz.com

SEE WHAT'S BEING STAGED
AT THE YALE REP

The Yale School of Drama (now known as the David Geffen School of Drama at Yale University after a $150 million donation) has a noteworthy professional theater in residence. The Yale Repertory Theatre has launched 17 Broadway shows that earned 10 Tony Awards and 40 nominations, and the theater itself received a Tony Award for Outstanding Regional Theater. It has premiered more than 100 productions since 1966, two of which won the Pulitzer Prize. When you put together quality scripts—some incubated through Yale's Binger Center for New Theatre—with the school's theater professionals and talented drama students, you get home runs. Keep your production notes because you might be seeing a future Meryl Streep or Liev Schreiber, both graduates of the program.

1120 Chapel St., New Haven, 203-432-1234
yalerep.org

CHILL OUT
WITH CHAMBER MUSIC

There must be something in the water in northwestern Connecticut for residents to have produced two highly regarded, long-standing chamber music festivals in such close proximity. Ellen Battell Stoeckel held chamber music and choral performances in a Music Shed on her Norfolk property in the early 1900s. Concerts are still held there today (but now there's air-conditioning) where luminaries like Sergei Rachmaninoff and Jean Sibelius performed. When Stoeckel died, her estate went to Yale, which now pairs gifted students with professional musicians at the Norfolk Chamber Music Festival–Yale Summer School of Music.

In nearby Falls Village, the acoustically perfect Gordon Hall is the setting for Music Mountain performances. Designed with hollow spaces under the floors and behind the walls to facilitate maximum music vibration, similar to a violin, the venue is listed on the National Register of Historic Places. Chamber music, as well as other genres like Dixieland jazz, has been played in this serene setting since 1930.

Norfolk Chamber Music Festival
Music Shed, Ellen Battell Stoeckel Estate, Rtes. 44 & 272, Norfolk
860-542-3000, norfolkmusic.org

Music Mountain
225 Music Mountain Rd., Falls Village
860-824-7126, musicmountain.org

TAKE IN A SHOW
AT THE O'NEILL

Named for the playwright who won a Nobel Prize in Literature and four Pulitzers (and lived in nearby New London), the Eugene O'Neill Theater Center has premiered a litany of well-known plays and musicals including *The House Of Blue Leaves*, *In the Heights*, three by August Wilson, and *Avenue Q*. This list is indicative of the broad range of material that's staged at this theater that has itself won two Tonys and received the National Medal of Arts from the White House. Founded in 1964, the O'Neill runs the National Theater Institute, National Playwrights Conference, National Music Theater Conference, National Critics Institute, National Puppetry Conference, and the Cabaret and Performance Conference. Those interested in taking a deep dive into the theater's place in history should pick up *The O'Neill: The Transformation of Modern American Theater*, which has forewords by Michael Douglas and Meryl Streep.

305 Great Neck Rd., Waterford, 860-443-5378
theoneill.org

OPEN YOUR MIND
TO THE ART OF PUPPETRY IN STORRS

We often think of puppets as being entertainment exclusively for children, but puppetry is an art form and a practiced skill as the professors and students of the University of Connecticut's Puppet Arts program will attest. The only degree-conferring puppetry program of its kind in the United States graduates highly regarded puppet artists who head around the globe to work on the stage, at theme parks, and in film, television, and commercials. UConn stages productions from its puppetry program and the Department of Dramatic Arts at its Connecticut Repertory Theatre. Try to schedule your campus visit to include the school's Ballard Institute and Museum of Puppetry, which exhibits puppets from all over the world, presents events, and holds the country's foremost repository of puppetry audiovisual materials. Admission to the museum is free. UConn is a world center for puppetry, and both children and adults come from all over to see why.

Ballard Institute and Museum of Puppetry
1 Royce Cir., Ste. 101B, Storrs, 860-486-8580
bimp.uconn.edu

Connecticut Repertory Theatre
802 Bolton Rd., Unit 1127, Storrs, 860-486-2113
crt.uconn.edu

Essex Steam Train,
courtesy of Tom Nanos

SPORTS
AND RECREATION

CHEER ON
THE HUSKIES

In the highly competitive and crowded playing field of college sports, the University of Connecticut Huskies stand out. UConn Athletics has won 23 national championships in four sports, but basketball is the star. The women's basketball team has won a record 11 NCAA championships, and the men's team has won five. UConn is the only school in college basketball history to clinch both the NCAA Division I Men's and Women's Basketball National Championships in the same season—and they did it twice! The head coaches of both teams made history themselves by being inducted into the Naismith Memorial Basketball Hall of Fame while still active coaches. The teams play at both the 10,000-seat Gampel Pavilion on the Storrs campus and at the 16,000-seat XL Center in Hartford. Even if you have no connection to UConn, it's a thrill to watch games live, surrounded by thousands of fans enthusiastically demonstrating Huskies pride.

877-AT-UCONN
tickets.uconnhuskies.com/basketball

Gampel Pavilion
2098 Hillside Rd., Storrs

XL Center
1 Civic Center Plaza, Hartford
xlcenter.com

TRY YOUR LUCK
AT FOXWOODS

Quite a complex, the 2,000-acre Foxwoods Resort Casino in Mashantucket has four hotels (plus Great Wolf Lodge, opening in 2025), numerous restaurants including Wahlburgers and Gordon Ramsay's Hell's Kitchen, an outlet mall, spa, and theaters that attract headline entertainment like John Legend. There's a zip line, golf, bowling, and a multilevel go-kart track. Don't forget paint-your-own ceramics, an escape room, Dark Ride VR, and the massive Mashantucket Pequot Museum & Research Center where the highlight is walking through a realistically re-created historic Pequot village. Oh, and yes, Foxwoods has gambling—blackjack, poker, craps, and slot machines, just to name a few.

350 Trolley Line Blvd., Mashantucket
GPS Address: 39 Norwich-Westerly Rd., Ledyard, 1-800-369-9663
foxwoods.com

TIP
Somewhat smaller than Foxwoods and located in Uncasville, Mohegan Sun's amenities include two spas, a golf course, and—unlike Foxwoods—an activity center where kids can participate in age-appropriate supervised activities while parents go off on their own. The two casinos are 15 minutes apart.

SPEND A DAY
AT THE BEACH AT HAMMONASSET

With 113 miles of Long Island Sound shoreline, Connecticut does not lack beaches. Many towns limit access to theirs, but if you're up for a beach day, head to the state's largest shoreline park. There are 1,000 acres to explore including two miles of beach at Madison's Hammonasset Beach State Park. Walk the boardwalk, enjoy a picnic with expansive views and fresh salt breezes, and don't skip Meigs Point Nature Center. Check ahead to see what's happening at this environmental learning center, which offers nature walks, wildlife presentations, and special events like Family Astronomy Night. There's a touch tank and displays that include about 50 species of local wildlife like turtles, snakes, amphibians, crabs, and fish. Set out for a hike on 5.7 miles of trails, reserve one of 550 grassy campsites and cabins, go biking or fishing, or even scuba dive! Hammonasset Park is a great place to spend quality time in nature with friends and family.

1288 Boston Post Rd., Madison, 203-245-8743
meigspointnaturecenter.org

portal.ct.gov/deep/state-parks/parks/hammonasset-beach-state-park/overview

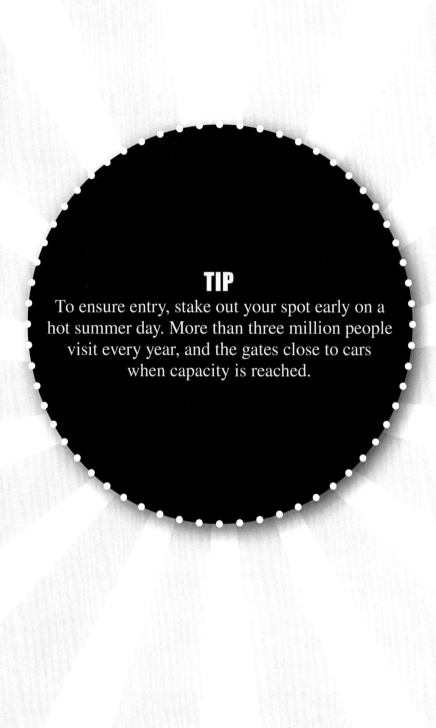

TIP

To ensure entry, stake out your spot early on a hot summer day. More than three million people visit every year, and the gates close to cars when capacity is reached.

GET OUT ON THE WATER
IN ESSEX

Picturesque marinas bustle in summer in Connecticut with boats of all shapes and sizes. From the water, the landscape seems idyllic—beautiful homes with rolling lawns, hillsides dotted with church steeples, and salt marshes where birds scan the still water for fish. If you don't have a boat, try the Airbnb-like app called GetMyBoat.com or reserve any number of marine experiences directly. Fish for striped bass, pedal a small barge, zip around in a two-person jet boat, paddle a canoe, or relax on the deck of a schooner. For a ride into the very beginnings of the state, head to the Connecticut River Museum in Essex to step aboard a replica of the historic *Onrust*. Six years before the *Mayflower* landed, Dutchman Adriaen Block sailed up the Connecticut River in the *Onrust,* and his exploration led to the establishment of a busy Dutch trading fort in what is now Hartford.

67 Main St., Essex, 860-767-8269
ctrivermuseum.org

TIP

There is also a replica of the world's first submarine at the Connecticut River Museum, and you can climb inside it. Called the *Turtle*, it was invented in 1776 and looks like a big wooden grenade.

SCREAM YOUR HEAD OFF
ON A LAKE COMPOUNCE
ROLLER COASTER

The fun at Lake Compounce Amusement Park, the oldest continuously operating amusement park in the United States, includes a famous wooden roller coaster. Hang on as you climb, drop, and zoom through the woods at 60 miles per hour on the 4,725-foot Boulder Dash, which opened in 2000. You can also loop the loop on the Zoomerang roller coaster or scream your head off on the 15-story, triple-launch Phobia Phear Coaster. If tamer rides are more your style, climb into a Flying Elephant, drive a mini classic car, or shoot ghosts with a laser gun. At the Crocodile Cove water park, float on a lazy river, plunge down a waterslide in a raft, and cool off in a water playground. Off season, look for special events like Phantom Fall Fest and Holiday Lights at this 332-acre park.

185 Enterprise Dr., Bristol, 860-583-3300
lakecompounce.com

TIP
The state's other amusement park, Quassy, in Middlebury, is easier to manage with small children. At 20 acres, it's a lot smaller while still offering rides, a lake, beach, boat rentals, water park, and arcade.

TAKE A
FALL FOLIAGE DRIVE
IN THE QUIET CORNER

On a glorious, crisp, bright, sunny fall day, driving country roads amid the splendor of vibrant foliage feeds the spirit. The Connecticut Department of Energy and Environmental Protection maintains a fall foliage report (depdata.ct.gov/forestry/foliage/foliagemap.htm) so you know where and when foliage is peaking. The department also suggests seven scenic leaf-peeping-loop routes. Their "Yankee Roots" loop (#4) travels approximately 100 miles through the Quiet Corner with its farms, rolling hills, and low-traffic roads. Begin in Vernon at Exit 67 of I-84; follow Route 31 south to Route 44; continue east to Route 195 where you travel south to Route 6; then turn east to Brooklyn and follow Route 169 north to North Woodstock; finally, go west on routes 197 and 190 back to I-84.

portal.ct.gov/deep/forestry/foliage/fall-foliage-driving-routes

TIP

Keep your eyes peeled for farm stands,
pumpkin patches, apple-picking opportunities,
breweries, and even a bison farm that offers
seasonal wagon rides and pumpkin painting.

Creamery Brook Bison
19 Purvis Rd., Brooklyn, 860-779-0837
creamerybrookbison.net

RELAX
ABOARD THE ESSEX STEAM TRAIN

An extremely enjoyable afternoon can be accomplished with very little effort aboard the Essex Steam Train & Riverboat, traveling into the heart of the Connecticut River Valley. Board a historic train at the 1892-era depot in Essex, and take in views of sailboats bobbing in harbors and kayakers paddling through marshes, interspersed with thick woods and charming homes. Disembark at Deep River to add a riverboat excursion to this 12-mile, one-hour train ride and you will find yourself steps away from the *Becky Thatcher*. Learn about the river's ecology, wildlife, and human history on a one-and-a-quarter-hour cruise, passing small boats and Jet Skiers and landmarks like Gillette Castle. Themed special events include dinner service, Mommy and Me afternoon tea, cigar and whiskey tastings, mystery evenings, and the ever-popular North Pole Express.

1 Railroad Ave., Essex, 860-767-0103
essexsteamtrain.com

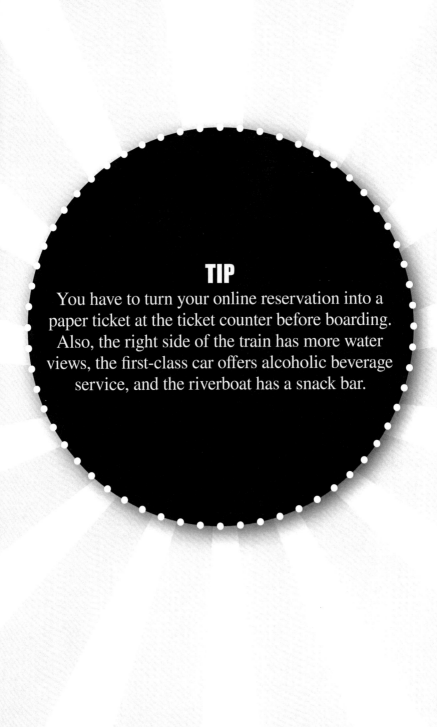

TIP

You have to turn your online reservation into a paper ticket at the ticket counter before boarding. Also, the right side of the train has more water views, the first-class car offers alcoholic beverage service, and the riverboat has a snack bar.

STOP TO SMELL THE ROSES
IN ELIZABETH PARK

Set an annual mid-June reminder to travel to Hartford's Elizabeth Park to promenade among thousands of roses. The Helen S. Kaman Rose Garden is the third largest of its kind in the United States. It has eight grass pathways where you can stroll—trying not to photobomb wedding pictures—on 2.5 acres blanketed with 15,000 rosebushes in 475 beds, reflecting 800 varieties of old and new roses. There are hybrid tea, climbers, floribunda, and pillar roses while ramblers brighten the arches of an extensive network of trellises. The entire park covers more than 100 acres where spring brings daffodils, tulips, and irises as a warm-up for the summer roses. With dahlia, herb, perennial, and rock gardens, there's usually something in bloom. Add a pond with ducks and geese, two gazebos, two playgrounds, trails, and a café, and you'll see why this beloved park has been a popular destination since it opened in 1897.

1561 Asylum Ave., West Hartford, 860-231-9443
elizabethparkct.org/garden/rose-garden

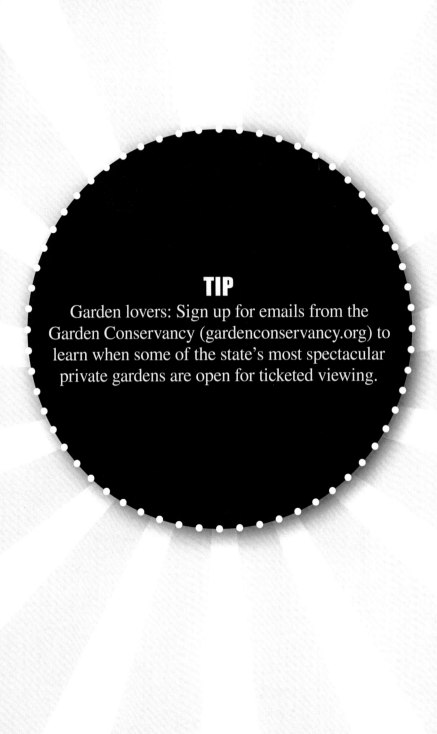

TIP

Garden lovers: Sign up for emails from the Garden Conservancy (gardenconservancy.org) to learn when some of the state's most spectacular private gardens are open for ticketed viewing.

DRIFT OVER THE COUNTRYSIDE
IN A HOT AIR BALLOON

Leaf peepers come to New England from all over the world to experience our foliage in its autumnal hues of burnt orange, crimson, and yellow gold. Imagine ditching roads, cars, and the Earth itself to float over swathes of fall-painted forest, iconic barns, and grazing cows. Climb into the basket and let Aer Blarney Balloons, operating out of Bethlehem, take you on a hot air balloon ride. You can help inflate the balloon if you wish or take a lesson in how to operate it. With pilots and balloons certified by the Federal Aviation Administration, Aer Blarney takes passengers on flights in colorful, 90-foot balloons at dusk or dawn when the winds are most calm over the Litchfield Hills, Housatonic River Valley, and central Connecticut. Add champagne and/or a private flight to make the occasion even more special.

92 Town Line Rd., Bethlehem, 203-910-4955
aerblarney.com

WITNESS THE SPORT OF KINGS
IN GREENWICH

Some of the world's most exciting high-goal polo is played on Sunday afternoons in the idyllic backcountry setting of the Greenwich Polo Club. Horses gallop at top speed across the field surrounded by smartly dressed spectators in the grandstand, under tents, and picnicking on the sidelines. The champagne flows and, at the halfway mark, people snack on treats from food trucks and wander onto the field—three times the length of a football field—to stomp divots. Polo is called the sport of kings because of its royal history, and you certainly feel like royalty in one of the wealthiest communities in the United States on Conyers Farm where the one-percenters reside in estates valued in the double-digit millions. Matches are family friendly and dogs on leashes are welcome.

1 Hurlingham Dr., Greenwich, 203-561-1639
greenwichpoloclub.com

TIP

In a converted barn on the polo grounds, the Brant Foundation Art Study Center (brantfoundation.org) is a small, free, by-appointment-only contemporary art museum that sometimes hosts open houses on match days.

EXPLORE THE THIMBLE ISLANDS
ABOARD *SEA MIST*

A picturesque archipelago of tiny, rocky islands dots the Connecticut shoreline, midcoast around Branford. Approximately two dozen of the Thimble Islands have homes, and all but one are private. Several companies offer tours in season from the charming hamlet of Stony Creek; 49-passenger *Sea Mist* is the longest-running—and the only boat with a Thimble Island Brewing Company IPA named after it. On a 45-minute cruise, hear tales of Captain Kidd's buried treasure, the wrath of hurricanes, people associated with the islands like President William Taft and General Tom Thumb, and how the area's granite was used in the base of the Statue of Liberty. Some of the seasonal homes are simple and others grand. Whether on stilts or sprawling with tennis courts and meticulously landscaped grounds, all have stunning 360-degree water views. Look for sea birds and seals as you meander around these lovely little islands.

GPS address: 4 Indian Point Rd., Branford, 203-488-8905
thimbleislandcruise.com

OTHER WAYS TO SEE THE THIMBLES

Thimble Island Kayak Rental
Call ahead to rent a kayak for a serene day on the water.
Be wary of rocks and bring a chart, compass, lunch,
and a waterproof bag.
Pickup and delivery at 1 Indian Point Rd., Stony Creek
203-859-0546, thimbleislandkayak.com

Stewart B. McKinney National Wildlife Refuge
On Outer Island, the farthest from shore, this refuge
is accessible to the public in season. It's a stop on the
Atlantic Flyway for seabirds like herons and egrets and
there's a scientific research center.
outerisland.org

HIKE ACROSS
A COVERED BRIDGE

Connecticut has been voted the best state for hiking based on factors including the number of hiking trails and waterfalls relative to state area and the percentage of land covered by parks. Bull's Bridge River Walk is a great choice for a hike as it passes one of Connecticut's iconic covered bridges, meets with the Appalachian Trail, and offers options for varying degrees of difficulty. In addition to the covered bridge, this river walk also includes scenic surprises like waterfalls, a small gorge, and an old power station. Fuel up in Kent before your walk or kick back afterwards with an artisanal hot cocoa or locally brewed beer.

248 Bulls Bridge Rd., South Kent
berkshirehiking.com/hikes/bulls_bridge.html

OTHER FAVORITE AREAS TO HIKE

Sleeping Giant State Park
The park's 32 miles of trails include the popular 1 1/2-mile
scenic trail that leads to the Mt. Carmel stone observation tower.
200 Mount Carmel Ave., Hamden
portal.ct.gov/deep/state-parks/parks/sleeping-giant-state-park

Devil's Hopyard State Park
Hike to Chapman Falls, which drop more than 60 feet.
366 Hopyard Rd., East Haddam
portal.ct.gov/deep/state-parks/parks/devils-hopyard-state-park

White Memorial Conservation Center
This 4,000-acre treasure has 35 miles of trails
and an engaging nature center.
80 Whitehall Rd., Litchfield
whitememorialcc.org

Talcott Mountain State Park
Climb 1,000 feet up to the 165-foot Heublein Tower
where several states are visible on a clear day.
GPS location: Summit Ridge Dr., Simsbury
portal.ct.gov/deep/state-parks/parks/talcott-mountain-state-park

BIKE
THE FARMINGTON CANAL

Once the longest in New England, the Farmington Canal connected seaports with inland towns to facilitate trade. Completed in 1835, it was superseded by the invention of the railroad, and later, the canal and barges were replaced by roads and trucks. Now, the 56 miles of the Farmington Canal Heritage Trail and the 18 miles of the Farmington River Trail are paved greenways that connect to even more walking and biking trails. The paths run through towns, farmland, and forests, and begin at Yale University in New Haven. Passing Hamden and Lake Whitney, Sleeping Giant State Park, and Southington, the Heritage Trail continues north to Farmington where you can stay on the canal trail or switch to the river trail and eventually reach the Massachusetts border.

Multipoint access, 860-202-3928
fchtrail.org

LUXURIATE IN A SPA DAY
IN WASHINGTON

Conjure an image of an ideal spa and then take a look at photos of the Well at Mayflower Inn to see if they match up. In beautiful Washington, the Mayflower is a sublimely elegant resort with indoor and outdoor pools, sophisticated dining, beautiful gardens, a putting green, and tennis courts. Its stunning destination spa welcomes guests with floor-to-ceiling windows that bring the forest into the heavenly white, high-ceilinged space. Specializing in bodywork that focuses on lymphatic drainage, it offers Reiki, acupuncture, and craniosacral massage as well as the more traditional Swedish, hot stone, and deep tissue massage. Extend your experience with one of their daily classes like barre, pool training, or meditation; you can even engage a health coach. Your blood pressure will drop just entering this serene space.

118 Woodbury Rd./Rte. 47, Washington, 860-619-7016
aubergeresorts.com/mayflower/wellness/the-well

INDULGE YOUR NEED FOR SPEED
AT LIME ROCK

If Connecticut's open country roads inspire a need for speed, head to a track. Lime Rock Park, a classic 1.53-mile, seven-turn course, is a popular venue for racing events and welcomes nonprofessionals with a variety of options. You can take your own car onto the track or rent a high-performance vehicle. If you complete the Driving Academy at the Skip Barber Racing School headquartered here, you can move on to the One Day Formula Racing School and take a Mygale Formula 4 race car for a spin. In the beautiful Litchfield Hills, Lime Rock is a beloved venue for car enthusiasts, whether cheering on races as spectators or channeling Mario Andretti themselves.

60 White Hollow Rd., Lakeville, 860-435-5000
limerock.com

TIP
From the Concours d'Elegance in Greenwich to Southington's Drive-In Classic Car Show and Summer Cruise Nights at the Sycamore Drive-In in Bethel, there are many opportunities to show off and admire notable automobiles in Connecticut. Carsandcoffeeevents.com is a useful resource.

IT SEEMS NUTMEGGERS (CONNECTICUT RESIDENTS) LIKE SPEEDING. HERE ARE OTHER PLACES TO FEEL THE THRILL OF RACING. BRING EAR PROTECTION.

New London-Waterford Speedbowl
You can drive your own vehicle at the New London-Waterford Speedbowl, a three-eighths-mile asphalt oval that hosts short track racing on Wednesday and Saturday nights from May to October.
1080 Hartford Rd./Rte. 85, Waterford, 860-574-9010
speedbowl.com

Thompson Speedway
If you'd like to sit behind the wheel of a Lamborghini Huracán LP610-4 or another exotic supercar, the staff at Thompson Speedway can make that happen.
205 E Thompson Rd., Thompson, 866-273-7727
thextremexperience.com/tracks/connecticut-thompson-speedway

Stafford Motor Speedway
There are racing events on Fridays at Stafford Motor Speedway, a half-mile oval asphalt track that's home of the SK Modified®.
55 West St., Stafford Springs, 860-684-2783
staffordmotorspeedway.com

PET A SHARK
AT THE MYSTIC AQUARIUM

You wouldn't expect parents to encourage their children to stick their hands into a big tank full of circling sharks, but this is one of the many interactive experiences that makes a visit to the Mystic Aquarium so memorable. Throughout the aquarium there are opportunities for hands-on experiences like petting an epaulette shark, feeding a cownose ray, and touching a sea star and hermit crab all while learning about the animals from the well-trained aquarium staff. Other highlights include daily sea lion shows, African penguins, beluga whales, 4-D movies, animatronic dinosaurs, and a VR experience that makes it feel like you're swimming with humpback whales. Visitors with more time and money could book a "Behind the Seas" tour or a special encounter with penguins, sea lions, reptiles, rays, or jellyfish. For a unique souvenir that's sure to be a conversation starter, arrange for a sea lion, ray, or whale to paint you a picture (not kidding).

55 Coogan Blvd., Mystic, 860-572-5955
mysticaquarium.org

TIP

For a regional attraction, the Maritime Aquarium impresses with sharks, sea turtles, meerkats, an IMAX theater, and touch tanks for rays, jellyfish, and sturgeon.

10 N Water St., Norwalk, 203-852-0700
maritimeaquarium.org

TAKE YOURSELF OUT
TO A YARD GOATS BALL GAME

If you like baseball, baby goats, and a dancing grounds crew, head to Hartford's Dunkin' Donuts Park for a Yard Goats game. The Double-A affiliate of the Colorado Rockies, the Yard Goats were founded in 2016 (after a history of other locations and affiliations) and are now part of the Eastern League. They didn't play one game of their inaugural season at their newly built stadium because it ran into construction issues, but fans have demonstrated that it was worth the wait. The park regularly sells out its 6,000 seats, and *Ballpark Digest* has named it the best AA stadium four times in its short history. The team's primary colors are blue and green, which are reflected in the colors of its goat mascots, Chompers and Chew Chew. Come on a Sunday afternoon to see real goats in the Goat Pen. Other special stadium features include a kids' play area, local craft beers, and a rotation of food carts featuring Hartford restaurants.

1214 Main St., Hartford, 860-240-5591
milb.com/hartford/ballpark

CLIMB THROUGH THE TREETOPS
AT THE ADVENTURE PARK AT STORRS

Get a shot of adrenaline by following a treetop trail. After a safety briefing that involves donning a harness, choose one of nine treetop trails and start your journey at the Adventure Park at Storrs. Travel on ropes courses, sail through the canopy on a zip line, and pause to take in a bird's-eye view of the forest from 106 treetop platforms. There are self-guided courses for anyone age 7 and older varying from the purple beginner trail to the thrill-packed double black diamond. Climb in fall to be surrounded by golden hues; fall also brings Firepit Fridays and the Halloween version of Glow in the Park. If you think it's exciting to zip-line during the day, try it at night in the dark! Guided by fairy lights, navigate the treetop courses to the sound of party music. Around Halloween, zip past glow-in-the-dark tombstones and other ghoulish decorations.

2007 Storrs Rd., Storrs, 860-946-0606
myadventurepark.com/sap

CROSS-COUNTRY SKI
IN THE SILENT SERENITY
OF THE FARMINGTON WOODS

Nordic skiers will be the first to tell you how the slow pace of gliding through the woods keeps you present in the moment, taking in the beauty of the forest and hearing the crunch of the snow. The state's only full-service cross-country ski center is Winding Trails, whose 12 miles of wide, double-tracked trails are well marked and vary in difficulty, with both gentle rolling terrain and steep hills with panoramic views of the center's 350 acres and beyond. You can rent skis here, take a lesson, grab a snack, and/or warm up by the fireplace. The trails are rolled, packed, and set with tracks to make it easy to click into your skis and go. Plus, trails are restricted to cross-country skiers so they won't be crowded with hikers or trampled by dogs. Nonskiers note: there's also a 150-foot hill with a 20-degree slope for sledding and tubing.

50 Winding Trails Dr., Farmington, 860-674-4227
windingtrails.org

TIP
Winding Trails is a membership organization; nonmembers must purchase a trail pass in advance.

GIDDYUP ON A FOREST TRAIL RIDE
IN EASTON

With so many wooded areas and so many farms, you'd think that there would be plenty of places for the public to go horseback riding, but you'd be wrong. Many stables board horses that you can only ride if you're the owner. If you'd love to ride in a private wooded trail system traversing 130 acres, there's only one place to go. Fairfield County's Gold Rush Farms is a horse farm that brings a little of the Old West to New England. But don't worry if you prefer English to Western as they will accommodate you. They also offer pony rides for kids and general riding lessons as well as instruction in horsemanship, gymkhana, jumping, and almost anything else horse related. And if you're looking for a fun party idea, book a Bonfire Night: a trail ride, barbeque, and bonfire all rolled into one Western-style event. Giddyup!

5 Silver Hill Rd., Easton, 203-268-9994
goldrushfarmsct.com

TIP
To book a ride, don't call ahead as they don't take reservations. Instead, call at 8 a.m. the morning of the day you'd like to ride to get a time slot. They are closed on Tuesdays, holidays, and the week after Labor Day.

WALK AMONG DINOSAURS
AT DINOSAUR PLACE

Heaven for a dinosaur-loving kid, Dinosaur Place is literally a prehistoric playground. Kids can climb up a Pachyrhinosaurus, a T-Rex Tower, or a huge web. Play mini-golf, navigate a maze, or cool off at the splash pad (bring a bathing suit and water shoes). Look up in wonder at the 50 life-size dinosaurs along one-and-a-half miles of wide, flat, wooded trails (fine for strollers). The 60-acre site also has indoor activities, a lunch spot, and a volcano that erupts on cue. Don't leave all this dino fun to children—bring a group and blow up your Instagram feeds with dinosaur selfies.

1650 Hartford-New London Tpke., Oakdale, 860-443-4367
naturesartvillage.com/experience/the-dinosaur-place

TIP

A construction crew uncovered 2,600 dinosaur footprints on a Rocky Hill site that's now a state park. One of the world's largest dinosaur trackways lies under Dinosaur State Park's geodesic dome surrounded by models of dinosaurs and interactive exhibits.
400 West St., Rocky Hill, 860-529-5816
dinosaurstatepark.org

FAWN OVER BABY ANIMALS
AT THE ZOO

Spring ushers in a whole new level of cuteness at Connecticut's Beardsley Zoo. The type and number of baby animals that make their debuts every year can't be guaranteed, but recent years have brought the birth of river otters and guinea hogs. The most celebrated arrivals have included endangered species such as Amur tigers, Amur leopards, a golden lion tamarin monkey, maned and red wolves, and three giant anteaters. The state's only zoo, Beardsley is small enough to be manageable but has enough variety of habitats and animals to be engaging. Opened in 1922, the zoo now has more than 350 animals including a peccary and rhea in Pampas Plains; an alligator and sandhill crane in Alligator Alley; an Andean bear and red panda on the Back Trail; and tropical wildlife like an agouti, scarlet ibis, sloth, and various species of reptiles and amphibians in the Rainforest Building.

1875 Noble Ave., Bridgeport, 203-394-6565
beardsleyzoo.org

STAND IN A FIELD OF SUNFLOWERS
IN GRISWOLD

Of course it will be an Instagram win, but standing in a field of sunflowers, tulips, or lavender will also feed your soul. In mid-July, 14 acres of sunflowers produce 300,000 blooms at Griswold's Buttonwood Farm. You can cut your own and pay $3 per flower, which the farm donates to the Make-A-Wish Foundation of Connecticut. After checking out, try the farm-produced ice cream at the on-site stand—a tasty bonus. Check their website or social media posts for updates on blooms, and bring your own bucket and shears to facilitate your visit and be more eco-conscious.

473 Shetucket Tnpke., Griswold, 860-376-4081
buttonwoodfarmicecream.com/sunflowers-for-wishes

OTHER PICK-YOUR-OWN FLOWER OPPORTUNITIES

Wicked Tulips Flower Farm
For a few weeks in April and May, Wicked Tulips Flower Farm opens its colorful fields for people to pick their own tulips.
382 Rte. 164, Preston, 401-297-3700
wickedtulips.com/pages/preston-ct-tulip-farm

Lavender Pond Farm
Over in the Quiet Corner, 10,000 lavender plants bloom in June and July at Lavender Pond Farm. A feast for the senses, the 25-acre farm has chickens and bees, a pond and covered bridge, cornhole games, and a small motorized train.
318 Roast Meat Hill Rd., Killingworth, 203-350-0367
lavenderpondfarm.com

Connecticut ballooning in Kensington,
courtesy of the Connecticut Office of Tourism

Lavender Pond Farm in Killingworth,
courtesy of the Connecticut Office of Tourism

Greenwich shopping,
courtesy of the Connecticut Office of Tourism

VersoFest,
courtesy of Anastasia Mills Healy

Goodspeed Opera House,
courtesy of Julie Balfour LLC

1876

Greenwich Polo East Coast Open,
courtesy of Andrew Werner

Christian Vincent Siriano Bridal Show,
courtesy of the Connecticut Office of Tourism

Aquila's Nest,
courtesy of Aquila's Nest Vineyard

Lake Compounce Amusement Park,
courtesy of the Connecticut Office of Tourism

Yale University Art Gallery in New Haven,
courtesy of the Connecticut Office of Tourism

Seaside Park in Bridgeport, courtesy of the Connecticut Office of Tourism

The Glass House in New Canaan,
courtesy of the Connecticut Office of Tourism

Sleeping Giant State Park in Hamden,
courtesy of the Connecticut Office of Tourism

Dinosaur Place,
courtesy of Anastasia Mills Healy

CULTURE
AND HISTORY

LOSE YOURSELF IN LANDSCAPES
AT THE WADSWORTH ATHENEUM

Connecticut's answer to the Met, Hartford's Wadsworth Atheneum is America's oldest art museum, housing impressive collections of everything from Roman antiquities to Joan Miró paintings and Colt firearms to Ballets Russes costumes. Get ready to lose yourself in landscapes: Frederic Church was from Hartford, and his paintings are well represented in the notable Hudson River School gallery. A destination in itself, the Amistad Center for Art & Culture is a separate nonprofit housed on the second floor (but with no separate entry fee). Created to document the African American experience, its moving exhibitions include slave shackles and a photo of Marian Anderson singing at the Lincoln Memorial in 1939. The largest item in the Wadsworth's collection is the nearby mansion of the museum's former director. At 86 feet long and 18 feet deep with one rococo floor and another decorated in an avant-garde modern style, the Austin House is certainly unique.

600 Main St., Hartford, 860-278-2670
thewadsworth.org

TOUR
THE STATE CAPITOL

Anyone can make an appointment for a free tour of our beautiful 1878-era State Capitol through the League of Women Voters. Look for the gold leaf dome at the edge of Bushnell Park—you can tell that the building's architect specialized in cathedrals with its soaring rotunda, Connecticut marble floors, and High Victorian Gothic decorative touches. Did you know that every state received a replica of the Liberty Bell in 1950? Ours is here along with other unique historical memorabilia like flags carried into battle by Connecticut soldiers, the plaster model of the *Genius of Connecticut* bronze statue atop the Capitol, and statues of our state heroine and hero, Prudence Crandall and Nathan Hale. You can also view the ornate house and senate chambers, learn about the legislative process, and see who has been inducted into the Connecticut Hall of Fame.

210 Capitol Ave., Hartford, 860-240-0222
cga.ct.gov/capitoltours

ENTER
A RARE PRISON-MINE

America's first state prison was an abandoned copper mine. While the Revolutionary War was raging, colonial leaders who were looking to save money on building a prison to incarcerate Tories and thieves jumped at the chance to stow them 75 feet underground. From 1773 to 1827, Old Newgate housed prisoners, at first exclusively in the mine. There were no toilet facilities, light, heat, or even guards at the beginning. (However, when the prisoners kept escaping, that changed.) It was always damp and cold (52 degrees), and insects and other critters were constant problems. Eventually, buildings were erected aboveground for both housing and workshops where inmates produced nails and barrels and milled grain with human horsepower. Today, the site is overseen by the state. You can take a guided tour of the mine and wander around the grounds to explore informative exhibits at this one-of-a-kind attraction.

115 Newgate Rd., East Granby, 860-653-3563
portal.ct.gov/ecd-oldnewgate

BE IMMERSED IN THE STATE'S SEAFARING PAST
AT THE MYSTIC SEAPORT MUSEUM

This popular re-created 19th-century seafaring village is full of buildings to explore, like a one-room schoolhouse, a printing shop, and a cooperage, but the main draw is the boats. Climb aboard the *Charles W. Morgan*, America's last surviving whaler, which was launched in New Bedford in 1841. See the collection of ship figureheads and check for demonstrations like setting a sail and dropping an anchor. There are plenty of interactive experiences for kids, including a boat-themed play area and opportunities to build model boats and to take a horse-and-carriage ride. There's a building with a play kitchen and other child-friendly activities and even a small planetarium. In keeping with the nautical theme, there are opportunities to purchase tickets for outings on the Mystic River. You can choose either a captained steamboat or sailboat or take a rowboat, sailboat, or pedal boat out for a spin on your own.

Rte. 27, exit 90 off I-95, 860-572-5315
mysticseaport.org

TIP
If you're visiting on your birthday, let the ticket office know—birthday visitors get in free.

EXPLORE
ALL THINGS YALE

Not only is a tour of Yale University—with its gothic-style architecture and 300-year history—an engaging way to spend an hour, but its museums (which are free) are also well worth visiting. Come to the Yale University Art Gallery for van Goghs and Hoppers and don't miss the sculpture garden and rooftop terrace. This was architect Louis Kahn's first public commission, and it's across Chapel Street from his last—the Yale Center for British Art. Holding the largest collection of UK art outside the UK, it has art pieces from all the major players including Turner, Constable, and Gainsborough. Both the British art and Yale Peabody Museum will reopen in 2024 after yearslong renovations; kids big and small are especially looking forward to seeing the Peabody's dinosaur skeletons. And don't overlook the Beinecke Rare Book & Manuscript Library's inspiring building that displays a Gutenberg Bible and houses the papers of many notable people.

Yale University tours
149 Elm St., New Haven, 203-432-2300
visitorcenter.yale.edu/tours

Yale University Art Gallery
1111 Chapel St., New Haven, 203-432-0600
artgallery.yale.edu

Yale Center for British Art
1080 Chapel St., New Haven, 877-274-8278
britishart.yale.edu

Yale Peabody Museum
170 Whitney Ave., New Haven, 203-432-8987
yale.edu/peabody

Beinecke Rare Book & Manuscript Library
121 Wall St., New Haven, 203-432-2977
beinecke.library.yale.edu

LEARN THE SHERLOCK HOLMES CONNECTION
AT GILLETTE CASTLE

Built to look like a medieval castle by the eccentric actor William Gillette in the early 1900s, this unique home on a hill overlooking the Connecticut River is the centerpiece of a 184-acre state park. The 24-room mansion was customized by Gillette with intricate locks and doors, no two the same, and took 20 men five years to complete. Gillette conducted his own private three-mile narrow-gauge railroad on his property with passengers including Albert Einstein and Charlie Chaplin, threw birthday parties for his 17 cats, and included hidden stairwells and other surprises in his 14,000-square-foot home. He played Sherlock Holmes more than 1,300 times over the course of 33 years but Gillette was more than an actor. He wrote the first authorized Sherlock Holmes adaptation for the stage, came up with the catchphrase "Elementary, my dear fellow" (which evolved into " . . . my dear Watson"), and originated the character's deerstalker cap, curved pipe, and magnifying glass.

67 River Rd., East Haddam, 860-526-2336
gillettecastlefriends.org

DON'T THROW STONES
AT THE PHILIP JOHNSON GLASS HOUSE

You may look at a photo of the not-so-large Glass House and
wonder if it's worth a trip to New Canaan. It is. The house is
part of a compound that includes a light-filled sculpture gallery,
a bunker-esque painting gallery with rotating exhibitions, and
a building with no right angles called Da Monsta. Johnson
dotted the magnificent 49-acre grounds with surprises like a
30-foot sculpture he liked to climb near a pond with a pavilion.
He designed the landscape, too, building bridges, digging the
pond, and cutting trees for perfect views. The house is open from
May to November, and tickets must be prebooked. Tours leave
from the Visitor Center in downtown New Canaan (leave time
to peruse the museum store), which is across the street from the
Metro-North station and surrounded by restaurants and shops.

Visitor Center
199 Elm St., New Canaan, 203-594-9884
theglasshouse.org

TIP
To continue the architectural pilgrimage, head to the nearby Grace
Farms, a free gathering place whose centerpiece is another lauded
glass-walled structure.
365 Lukes Wood Rd., New Canaan, 203-920-1702
gracefarms.org

WALK THROUGH
A NATIVE AMERICAN VILLAGE

The Mashantucket Pequot Museum & Research Center is an enormous, impressive museum near Foxwoods Resort Casino, on the Mashantucket Pequot Tribal Nation's reservation. The exhibits begin with faux glaciers overhead and a soundtrack of running water as an escalator deposits you into the Ice Age, when the story of the Native Americans of this region began. Move through time and learn about the customs, language, and history of the tribe through life-size exhibits like a caribou hunt from 11,000 years ago, dramatic films including one about the devastating 1637 Pequot War, and touch-screen, interactive computer presentations. One highlight of this museum is walking through a realistically re-created 16th-century village guided by an interactive audio tour. If the 185-foot observation tower is open, take the elevator by the main entrance for a fantastic view of the Foxwoods Resort surrounded by 2,000 acres of forest.

110 Pequot Trl., Mashantucket, 860-396-6910
pequotmuseum.org

TIP

A much smaller yet very worthwhile
Native American museum is the Institute for
American Indian Studies. Learn about customs
and traditions, how to measure the calendar year
with the shell of a snapping turtle, and stand in a
re-created Algonkian wigwam.

38 Curtis Rd., Washington, 860-868-0518
iaismuseum.org

CLIMB ABOARD
A PIONEERING SUBMARINE
IN GROTON

The only submarine museum managed by the US Navy, the free Submarine Force Library and Museum is the home of the USS *Nautilus*, the world's first nuclear-powered sub and the first vessel to reach 90 degrees north—the North Pole. She was built nearby and her missions took her around the globe, traveling half a million miles over 25 years. Not only can you climb inside to see what life was like for the more than 100 sailors aboard but you can also learn about the history of submarine technology and undersea exploration through exhibitions and interactive experiences. See what torpedoes and mines look like, catch a short documentary, embark on a scavenger hunt, and download an app for an augmented-reality experience: Point your phone's camera at something that interests you and more information appears—a technology that will engage kids and hold sub and military aficionados captive for hours.

1 Crystal Lake Rd., Groton, 800-343-0079
ussnautilus.org

STEP INSIDE A JEWEL BOX
AT THE FISH CHURCH

There is no more ethereal place to be on a sunny Sunday morning than the balcony of the First Presbyterian Church of Stamford. Modernist architect Wallace Harrison, whose projects also included Radio City Music Hall and the United Nations headquarters, successfully set out to emulate the stained glass experience of European cathedrals like Sainte-Chapelle in Paris. He chose 86 hues of stained glass and placed 20,000 pieces in 152 panels using a mosaiclike method called dalle de verre. In an impressive feat of engineering, he installed these concrete panels at 74–78 degree tilts, which allowed him to build the soaring sanctuary without columns or buttresses so there would be no obstruction to prevent the sun's rays from bathing the pews in soft, multicolored light. "Have you ever thought what it would be like to live inside a giant sapphire?" Harrison once asked.

1101 Bedford St., Stamford, 203-324-9522
fishchurch.org

TIP
This church is nicknamed the Fish Church because of the fish-shaped floor plan. However, that was apparently not Harrison's intent. The expanded space in the rear was simply intended to enhance acoustics.

· ·

UNDERSTAND THE FASCINATING LIFE OF A LITERARY ICON
AT MARK TWAIN'S HOUSE

One of America's most celebrated authors, Samuel Clemens/ Mark Twain lived in a 25-room High Gothic Victorian mansion in Hartford with his family from 1874 to 1891. He wrote the rural Southern exploits of his beloved characters Tom Sawyer and Huckleberry Finn in his third-floor office, which doubled as a billiard room. Today, this mansion provides lively themed tours to illustrate Twain's life, like the one that takes visitors behind the scenes with Twain's in-character butler. Interior design buffs will be interested by the work of Louis Comfort Tiffany's design firm Associated Artists. For the context it provides, visit the separate museum at the Twain House before taking a house tour. The museum showcases artifacts like the author's iconic glasses and his failed printing invention, and it's worthwhile to watch the informative 23-minute Ken Burns documentary that's played on a continuous loop throughout the day.

351 Farmington Ave., Hartford, 860-247-0998
marktwainhouse.org

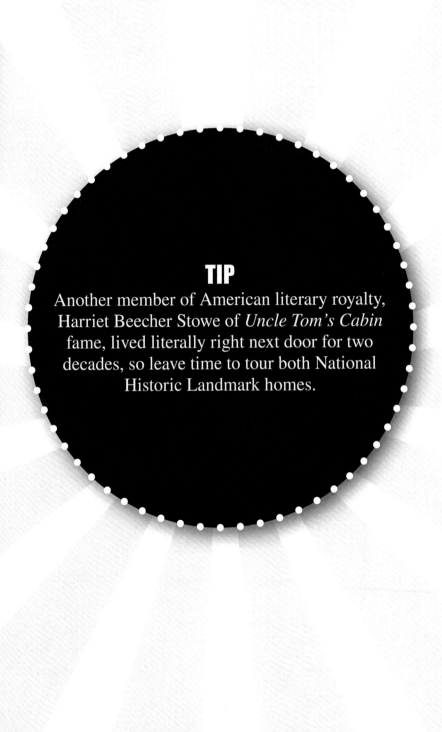

TIP

Another member of American literary royalty, Harriet Beecher Stowe of *Uncle Tom's Cabin* fame, lived literally right next door for two decades, so leave time to tour both National Historic Landmark homes.

EDUCATE YOURSELF
ABOUT THE STATE'S
AFRICAN AMERICAN HISTORY

The more than 100 sites in upwards of 50 towns on the Connecticut Freedom Trail tell the inspiring and often harrowing stories of African Americans in the state. See where Marian Anderson and Paul Robeson lived, locate a statue of Jackie Robinson, and honor the lives of other pioneering Black Americans at churches, cemeteries, and monuments. Many sites on the trail are connected to one of the most important cases in the struggle toward abolishing slavery in the United States—that of the African captives who commandeered *La Amistad*. A dramatic series of events resulted in their imprisonment and trials in Connecticut. Residents raised national awareness and funds for their defense, and when their release was secured in 1841 by former US President John Quincy Adams at a pivotal US Supreme Court trial, they housed and educated the Africans until their safe passage back to Sierra Leone.

Various locations statewide
ctfreedomtrail.org

TIPS
For background, watch Steven Spielberg's 1997 film *Amistad*.
For a comprehensive list of Amistad-related sites in the state, see ctfreedomtrail.org/trail/amistad/sites.

SAVE A TRIP TO FRANCE
AT THE HILL-STEAD MUSEUM

The renowned French Impressionist collection at the Hill-Stead Museum was the prescient work of Alfred Pope who traveled frequently to France and collected the paintings of Degas, Monet, and Manet during their lifetimes when Impressionism was widely scorned. His teenage daughter Theodate, who became one the country's first female architects, submitted plans to McKim, Mead & White for her family's lovely 1901 estate. It's not often that you have the opportunity to admire three renowned paintings in a suburban living room decorated with Duncan Phyfe furniture and Ming dynasty porcelain. Explore the stately 152-acre grounds with a Beatrix Farrand–designed sunken garden, walking trails that traverse woodlands and meadows, and a flock of resident sheep. Keep an eye out for special events like poetry readings and dance performances.

35 Mountain Rd., Farmington, 860-677-4787
hillstead.org

EMERGE FROM THE MUSEUM OF CONNECTICUT HISTORY
A MORE INFORMED RESIDENT

The free Museum of Connecticut History, in the building that houses the state supreme court and state library, is a comprehensive repository of artifacts focusing on the development of Connecticut's government and industries. Learn the story of why the 1662 royal charter granting rights to colonists was hidden in the Charter Oak tree and see the original charter and items made from the tree, which was felled by a storm. Peruse a renowned collection of firearms manufactured by Colt and see rare coins like the Higley Copper token, which was the first coin minted in America in 1737. State residents have invented countless noteworthy devices and started well-known global companies over the years. Here you can learn about the patents filed for the helicopter, sewing machine, Wiffle ball, can opener, and many other Connecticut-made things that are still part of the fabric of our society.

231 Capitol Ave., Hartford, 860-757-6535
museumofcthistory.org

TRY YOUR HAND
AT PLEIN AIR PAINTING AT THE FLO GRIS

Around the turn of the last century, Florence Griswold operated a boarding house that attracted American Impressionist painters including Childe Hassam. The site of the yellow Georgian home on 12 acres along the Lieutenant River inspired many artworks. Known for her stunning gardens, Miss Florence planted peonies, irises, roses, violets, lavender, and lilies, along with other flowers. Historically accurate today, these beautiful gardens have been painstakingly re-created for public enjoyment. On Sunday afternoons in the summer, admission includes painting supplies, and visitors are encouraged to paint en plein air as members of the Lyme Art Colony did. First tour the old house, then see the exhibits in the modern gallery before heading over to the Hartman Education Center to pick up a folding stool, smock, brushes, paint-filled palette, and small canvas. Then compare your masterpiece with theirs and stand in awe of their talent.

Florence Griswold Museum
96 Lyme St., Old Lyme, 860-434-5542
florencegriswoldmuseum.org

LET AIRCRAFT TELL THEIR STORIES
AT THE NEW ENGLAND AIR MUSEUM

A massive aviation museum next to Bradley International Airport, the New England Air Museum displays more than 80 aircraft ranging from helicopters to supersonic jets. See the Boeing B-29 Superfortress that dropped the atomic bombs on both Hiroshima and Nagasaki in 1945. Have the rare opportunity to peek into the control car of the anti-submarine patrol craft, the Goodyear ZNPK-28 blimp; it and the Sikorsky VS-44A *Excambian* four-engine Flying Boat are the last of their kind. *Excambian*'s many lives include transatlantic military service during World War II, taking Catalina tourists sightseeing, and even serving as a hot dog stand in the Virgin Islands after it lost operational ability. The museum also offers flight simulators so realistic that some are used for pilot instrument training.

36 Perimeter Rd. (off Rte. 75), Windsor Locks, 860-623-3305
neam.org

TWO OTHER AEROSPACE MUSEUMS

Connecticut Air & Space Center
225 B Main St., Stratford, 203-345-1559
ctairandspace.org

National Helicopter Museum
2480 Main St., Stratford, 203-375-8857
nationalhelicoptermuseum.org

DISCOVER AN ENVIABLE REPOSITORY OF AMERICAN ART
IN NEW BRITAIN

Connecticut is a state of many firsts, some surprising. If you stopped people on the street across America and asked them to guess the location of the first museum in the country dedicated to American art, few would say New Britain, Connecticut. Founded in 1903 and now holding an abundance of renowned works, the New Britain Museum of American Art is a gem. Pieces here stretch from colonial portraits to Ashcan School works and from Hudson River School landscapes to Chihuly glass. Major artists like Mary Cassatt, Winslow Homer, Georgia O'Keeffe, Robert Motherwell, and Andy Warhol are represented, and fans of illustration will linger at works by Norman Rockwell and Maxfield Parrish. Another important holding is the mural series, *The Arts of Life in America* by Thomas Hart Benton, the first artist to make the cover of *Time* (1934).

56 Lexington St., New Britain, 860-229-0257
nbmaa.org

TIP
New Britain native Sol LeWitt's first
museum show was here in 1949 as part of a
Young Talent exhibition; now NBMAA has
hundreds of his works.

TOUR AMERICA'S FIRST MANSION
IN NORWALK

LeGrand Lockwood constructed America's first mansion in 1868 with a 42-foot rotunda, murals of frolicking Cupids, and a Moorish Room. When his good fortune reversed (Lockwood died only four years after moving in), the Mathews family lived here until 1938. Noteworthy in scale and ambition, the 62-room Lockwood-Mathews Mansion is an imposing mix of Victorian, French Château, and Scottish Manor architecture with an interior richly decorated with frescoes, gilt, and marble. Although closed for renovations until fall 2024, the museum holds interesting talks and an annual flea market and usually has rotating exhibitions.

295 West Ave., Norwalk, 203-838-9799
lockwoodmathewsmansion.com

TIP

If you've seen either of the two *Stepford Wives* movies, the home is the setting for the Stepford Men's Club where the husbands transform their wives into robots.

SEE WHERE IT ALL BEGAN
AT THE OLD STATE HOUSE

Walk through 400 years of history in Hartford's Old State House, the Charles Bulfinch–designed former state capitol built in 1796. The lower floor provides a wonderful overview of the state's many inventions, famous residents, and notable accomplishments. On the upper floors, see the courtroom where one of the Amistad trials happened, a Gilbert Stuart painting of George Washington, and a historic museum of curiosities like an enormous lobster claw and a two-headed calf. One of the first National Historic Landmarks, it stands on the site where Hartford founder Reverend Thomas Hooker delivered a sermon that inspired the Fundamental Orders of 1639. Arguably the world's first written constitution, it includes the concept of "the consent of the governed" that later appeared in the US Constitution.

800 Main St., Hartford, 860-522-6766
wp.cga.ct.gov/osh

LEARN THE ROLE CONNECTICUT PLAYED
IN THE LIFE OF MARTIN LUTHER KING JR.

Georgia and Alabama are closely associated with Martin Luther King Jr., but the seedling of the Civil Rights Movement he would eventually lead was planted in Connecticut. The first time he experienced life outside the segregated South, he was in Simsbury. King spent the summers of 1944 and 1947 picking tobacco for Cullman Brothers, one of many students at historically Black colleges in the South who earned money for school on Connecticut tobacco farms. King preached for the first time to 107 boys in his dorm, sang in the choir at First Church in Simsbury, and in letters home expressed wonder at the freedoms he experienced. Simsbury High School students produced a short documentary, *Summers of Freedom: The Story of Martin Luther King, Jr. in Connecticut* and lobbied for the Martin Luther King Jr. in Connecticut Memorial at the Simsbury Free Library.

Simsbury Free Library
749 Hopmeadow St., Simsbury, 860-408-1336

TIP
Other notable students in this college work program included Mahalia Jackson, Thurgood Marshall, and Arthur Ashe.

DISCOVER ELI WHITNEY'S OTHER REVOLUTIONARY INVENTION
IN HAMDEN

Schoolchildren learn that Eli Whitney invented the cotton gin but another of his game-changing inventions is not as well known. In manufacturing the cotton gin, he found that if workers made the same parts over and over again instead of building the entire machine, the process went faster. Whitney is now credited with constructing the first American factory because he applied this idea of using standardized, interchangeable machine-made parts and a division of labor to making weapons, and in 1798 the government gave him a contract for 10,000 firearms. Connecticut got the nickname Arsenal of the Nation during the Revolutionary War for supplying the Continental Army, and Whitney set the stage for other local weapons manufacturers to be established, like Colt and Winchester, and for the processes to be used in other mass production factories around the world.

The Eli Whitney Museum and Workshop
915 Whitney Ave., Hamden, 203-777-1833
eliwhitney.org

TAKE A WALK THROUGH THE STATE'S MILITARY HISTORY
IN WEST HAVEN

At the under-the-radar West Haven Veterans Museum and Learning Center, trace the state's military history through carefully selected memorabilia including firsthand written accounts of the Revolutionary War, a Civil War Union frock coat, and World War I doughboy uniforms. World War II stories are told through both Allied and Axis artifacts including the wing of an infamous Japanese Zero plane shot down by the Branford 211th antiaircraft artillery unit, a display of rations, and the wedding gown a bride made from the parachute that saved her groom. You can walk inside a bunker, sit in a Jeep with a 50-caliber mounted machine gun, and learn what a Gibson Girl transmitter did. In a replica of the New Haven Grays' elegant meeting room, learn about this unit that fought in 19 Civil War battles including the Battle of Bull Run and Gettysburg. Bonus: admission to this out-of-the-way gem is free.

30 Hood Terr., West Haven, 203-934-1111
whmilmuseum.org

FIND OUT ABOUT CONNECTICUT'S STATE HEROINE
AT THE PRUDENCE CRANDALL MUSEUM

Connecticut's state heroine was a White woman who taught Black girls in 1833. When Prudence Crandall opened the Canterbury Female Boarding School, just White girls attended. When she began admitting Black girls, White families pulled their daughters and Crandall made the radical decision to teach only Black girls. She recruited students with help from William Lloyd Garrison who provided letters of introduction to Black families in nearby states who could afford the $25 per quarter tuition. The White response was a new "Black Law" that made it illegal for Black people to cross state lines for education, which engendered three court cases. Intense furor from neighbors culminated in vigilante violence that closed the school. Although it was open for only a year, the school paved the way for other educators and abolitionists, and Crandall's court cases were referenced in arguments that eventually resulted in the 14th Amendment.

1 S Canterbury Rd., Canterbury, 860-546-7800
portal.ct.gov/decd/content/historic-preservation/04_state_museums/
prudence-crandall-museum

SEE CONNECTICUT'S STONEHENGE
AT HOGPEN HILL FARMS

One of the country's foremost data visualization experts erected 100 sculptures on his 234-acre property, which he opens to the public with advanced tickets. There are many striking sculptures at Edward Tufte's Hogpen Hill Farms including arrangements of massive stone monoliths that evoke Stonehenge. You can walk under an Airstream trailer that dangles 31 feet overhead or through four sizable stainless steel arches lined up like a Slinky half buried in the ground. On a stroll around the hilly property, pass large metal fish swinging from trees and a giant black inflatable swan floating in a small lake. Hike on five miles of wooded trails and follow the paths through a bamboo thicket. Pay attention to the signs, which are part of the unorthodox experience with instructions such as "Shut up and look."

100 Weekeepeemee Rd., Woodbury
edwardtufte.com/tufte/hogpen-hill-farms

TIP
Pack lunch—it's a gorgeous spot for a picnic and there's no food service on the property.

FIND OUT WHY NATHAN HALE
IS THE CONNECTICUT STATE HERO

A patriotic icon, Nathan Hale was born in a rambling red Georgian home on 17 acres in Coventry in 1755. After graduating from Yale with first-class honors, he became a schoolteacher and then joined the Continental Army like five of six of his brothers. In New York City, he bravely volunteered to gather information about British troop movements, becoming one of America's earliest spies. He was found out, and before he was hanged for treason in 1776, his alleged famous last words were "I only regret that I have but one life to lose for my country." At his very well-preserved home you can see what 18th-century life was like and attend special events like candlelight ghost tours and Revolutionary War encampments. The home borders the 1,500-acre Nathan Hale State Forest, but don't enter if it is hunting season.

2299 South St., Coventry, 860-742-6917
ctlandmarks.org/properties/nathan-hale-homestead

TIP
You can also visit two schoolhouses where Hale taught.
19 Atlantic St., New London, 860-873-3399
29 Main St., Rte. 149, East Haddam, 860-334-2858
sarconnecticut.org

EXPLORE THE CONNECTION
BETWEEN *THE GREAT GATSBY* AND WESTPORT

In the roaring '20s, Westport had a wild side. Not known for shying from debauchery, F. Scott and Zelda Fitzgerald honeymooned in Westport in 1920 and rented a cottage next to what is now Longshore Club Park. At the time, the 175-acre property on the Long Island Sound belonged to mystery multimillionaire Frederick E. Lewis. The Fitzgeralds could see across the bay where another grand estate had a lawn that rolled to a beach and a long dock with a green light. After years of research, two Westport residents provided strong evidence in a book and documentary that Westport is a setting for both of the Fitzgeralds' writings. Keep an eye out for tours organized through the Westport Historical Society to literally walk in the Fitzgeralds' footsteps and hear about the real-life characters and events that inspired Fitzgerald to write an American classic.

Longshore Club Park
260 Compo Rd. S, Westport

Westport Museum of History & Culture
203-222-1424
westporthistory.org

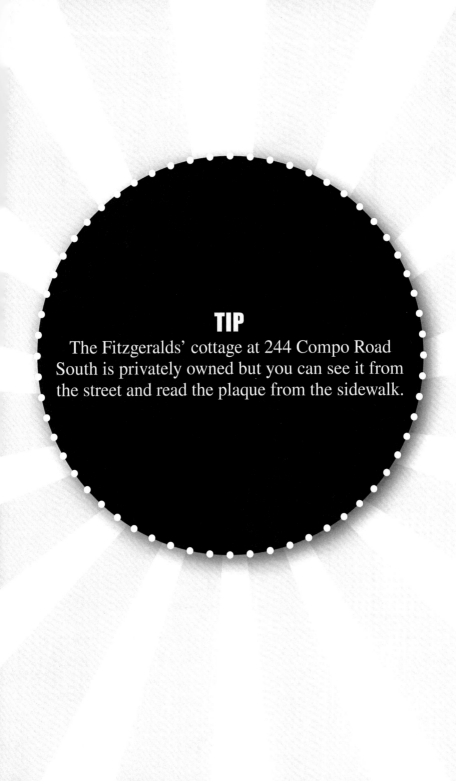

TIP

The Fitzgeralds' cottage at 244 Compo Road South is privately owned but you can see it from the street and read the plaque from the sidewalk.

GET INTO
THE HALLOWEEN SPIRIT
AT PLAINVILLE'S WITCH'S DUNGEON

Follow the creepy organ music coming from an industrial warehouse in Plainville to see a small but comprehensive museum of costumes, props, and memorabilia from classic monster movies. Walk among atmospheric tableaux featuring life-size figures from the golden age of horror and sci-fi cinema like Bela Lugosi, Boris Karloff, Lon Chaney, and Vincent Price. If the collection seems worthy of Hollywood, it's because it is. The museum's founder, Cortlandt Hull, is the great-nephew of the first cinematic lycanthrope (the headliner of the 1935 movie *Werewolf of London*). Obsessed with monster movies from a young age, he became a professional artist in the field and his connections enabled him to amass an outstanding collection that includes memorabilia from films like *Creature from the Black Lagoon*, *Bride of Frankenstein*, and *House of Wax*. The museum also displays life casts of actors and items from films outside the genre like E.T. on his bicycle.

103 E Main St., Plainville, 860-307-6095
preservehollywood.org

TIP
Arrive before opening to cut down time spent in line.

UNDERSTAND WHY GEORGE WASHINGTON WASN'T AMERICA'S FIRST PRESIDENT
IN SCOTLAND

Did you know that you can visit the home of America's first president in Connecticut? Not Mount Vernon but the Huntington Homestead. Samuel Huntington was technically president eight years before Washington under the country's first founding document, the Articles of Confederation. He was president of the Continental Congress when the founders outlined the government and officially named the country the United States of America. The US Constitution replaced the Articles of Confederation on March 4, 1789, and George Washington became president a month later. Born in Windham (now Scotland), Huntington was a self-taught lawyer who signed the Declaration of Independence and held various elected positions including governor of Connecticut for a decade in his later years. You can tour his 1723 birthplace, which is a National Historic Landmark, free of charge, and learn about this not-well-known slice of Connecticut history.

36 Huntington Rd./Rte. 14, Scotland, 860-423-1547
huntingtonhomestead.org

TOUR CONNECTICUT'S ANSWER TO NEWPORT'S MANSIONS
AT HARKNESS MEMORIAL PARK

The grand estate Eolia (named for the Greek god of wind), with its sweeping water views and gorgeous gardens, would fit right in alongside the famous "cottages" of Newport, Rhode Island. Set on 230 acres in what is now Harkness Memorial Park, the 1906 Roman Renaissance–style mansion was the summer residence of Edward and Mary Harkness. It has 20 bedrooms, 14 baths, and 11 fireplaces, and you can see special furnishings and decor throughout, like a Venetian glass chandelier in the dining room, a floral ceiling mural in the breakfast room, and a bathtub that could run both fresh and salt water. Beautiful gardens were designed by well-known landscape architects: Beatrix Farrand originally planned the formal gardens and decades later Marian Coffin updated the East Garden. Vines creep on a pergola, heliotrope releases its scent of vanilla, and color bursts continually from the thousands of plantings.

275 Great Neck Rd., Waterford, 860-437-1523
friendsofharkness.org

DELVE DEEP INTO WATERBURY AND BEYOND
AT THE MATTATUCK MUSEUM

A combination art museum, Connecticut cultural storyteller, and social gathering place, the Mattatuck Museum is worthy impetus for an outing in Waterbury. If you've never thought of buttons as art, you will after time spent studying the Matt's collection. Waterbury is home to America's oldest button producer, which donated 10,000 of these fasteners including ones made of jewels and hand-painted glass. Other collections focus on artists with Connecticut connections. The permanent collection includes works by Alexander Calder and Frederic Church, and 12 exhibits a year have featured Walter Wick of *I Spy* fame and Andy Warhol screen prints of endangered animals. A big, permanent history exhibit showcasing Waterbury includes clocks and a Nauga— the Naugahyde mascot.

144 W Main St., Waterbury, 203-753-0381
mattmuseum.org

EXPLORE THE LEGACY OF ISRAEL PUTNAM
IN REDDING

A legend in his own time, Israel Putnam was a farmer who killed the state's last wolf; a soldier who survived both capture by Native Americans and a shipwreck during the Seven Years' War; and a commander at the Battle of Bunker Hill, famous for reportedly saying, "Don't fire until you see the whites of their eyes." The Town of Putnam is named for him, and his surname emblazons numerous avenues, streets, and schools throughout the state. Learn about "Old Put" at Putnam Memorial State Park in Redding, on the site of the Continental Army's 1778–79 winter encampment. At an on-site museum see displays of artifacts that have been found here and/or walk the short trail that passes the remains of the encampment and reconstructed huts.

Rtes. 107 and 58, Redding, 203-938-2285
putnampark.org

OTHER SITES CONNECTED TO GENERAL ISRAEL PUTNAM

Knapp's Tavern/Putnam Cottage
243 E Putnam Ave., Greenwich, 475-889-5786
putnamcottage.org

"Wolf Den" cave in Mashamoquet Brook State Park
276 Mashamoquet Rd., Pomfret Center, 860-928-6121
portal.ct.gov/deep/state-parks/parks/mashamoquet-brook-state-park

Putnam equestrian monument holding the general's remains
Brooklyn Town Green, CT 169 near Winding Rd., Brooklyn

Putnam statue in Bushnell Park
Trinity St. near path to the Capitol, Hartford

A Pratt Street event in Hartford, courtesy of the Connecticut Office of Tourism

SHOPPING
AND FASHION

GET READY FOR A HUNT
AT ELEPHANT'S TRUNK FLEA MARKET

An open field in New Milford transforms into a shopping mecca on Sundays from April to December. Around since the '70s, Elephant's Trunk often features more than 500 vendors selling everything from vintage weathervanes to collectible comic books as well as some new items like hats and jewelry. Inspired by DIY shows (*Flea Market Flip* has been filmed here), industrious folks hunt for furniture with good bones to refurbish. Some vendors are regulars while others rotate so the thousands of shoppers every week never know what they're going to find. The early bird gets the worm here: Serious treasure hunters pay a premium to enter at 5:30 a.m., and the field is cleared by 3:30 p.m. Don't worry if browsing whets your appetite as you can pick up sustenance like a breakfast burrito, burger, fried chicken, and fresh-squeezed lemonade from a range of food vendors. There's also a farmers market on-site.

490 Danbury Rd., New Milford, 860-355-1448
etflea.com

TIP

Anyone with $60 can become a vendor, so clean out your attic and set up a folding table.

GO GOWN SHOPPING
AT CHRISTIAN SIRIANO

Many famous fashion designers like Oscar de la Renta and Diane von Furstenberg have had homes in Connecticut, but they didn't set up ateliers here. Enter wunderkind Christian Siriano who lives in Westport and has a showroom downtown at the Collective West. A luxury goods destination for clothing, interior decor, jewelry, and art, it also features a handful of other brands. You might know Siriano from winning *Project Runway* at the tender age of 21 or from dressing Kim Kardashian, Michelle Obama, and Lady Gaga. In addition to evening wear and head-turning cocktail dresses, you can find signed books, sketches, shoes, home goods, fragrances, and more. Follow @thecollective.west on Instagram to be in the know about new products, sample sales, art shows, and other events.

940 Post Rd. E, Westport, 203-349-5588
thecollective-west.com

LOSE TRACK OF TIME
AT PUTNAM'S ANTIQUES MARKETPLACE

In the old and preservation-minded Nutmeg State, it's not a shock to find a plethora of antiques dealers. There are countless stores on back roads across the state and on main streets in towns like Woodbury and Kent. Putnam is also a hotbed for antiques and collectibles, and Antiques Marketplace stands out for its sheer volume of goods. Four floors are packed with seemingly every item imaginable from every time period. It bills itself as an "antiques mega-mall," giving hundreds of dealers space to exhibit antique toys, costume jewelry, porcelain figurines, and vintage clothing as well as furniture, ephemera, fine art, and basically any other conceivable category. If you're on the hunt for silver coins, military memorabilia, a sequined clutch, or an old advertising sign, you're in luck. Don't venture in with a non-shopper as you will want to spend hours here.

109 Main St., Putnam, 860-928-0442
facebook.com/antiquesmarketplace

TIP

After browsing, stop for swordfish at
85 Main or a beer at the Crossings Brew Pub.

85 Main
85 Main St., Putnam, 860-928-1660
85main.com

The Crossings Restaurant & Brew Pub
45 Main St., Putnam, 860-928-3663
crossingsbrewpub.com

SHOW YOUR STATE PRIDE
AT HARTFORD PRINTS!

Pick up a cutting board in the shape of Connecticut, a "Small State Great Beer" pint glass, or a "CT QT" onesie for the baby in your life at this fun downtown gift store that designs its own apparel. For example: your favorite minimalist might jump at the chance to wear a hoodie with no words, just the Hartford skyline. Beyond the Connecticut-themed merchandise, there's plenty of stuff you never knew you needed, like a kit to make your own hard seltzer and a needlepoint kit that results in a canvas reading "This Took Forever." How about party plates in the shape of a disco ball or a Skittle Christmas tree ornament? You've gotta love a store that has a section for "flair" like buttons, coin purses, and key chains. You can also visit their outpost across from Starbucks in Bradley International Airport, or order online.

42 1/2 Pratt St., Hartford, 860-578-8447
hartfordprints.com

TIP

The store is on a pedestrian-only street near the XL Center where you could stumble across a free yoga class or a pop-up DJ.

RAISE A PADDLE
AT LITCHFIELD AUCTIONS

The excitement of previewing remarkable items, the anticipation of each lot, and the thrill of winning a bid—there's nothing like a live auction. The first auction that Litchfield Auctions held in 1994 contained a few hundred lots that sold for $100,000. Now it's not unusual for one of their events to have 1,000 lots fetching $1 million. They've handled unique items like a Tiffany daffodil vase and a statement steel and abalone table sourced from the estates of celebrities, artists, and scions of industry with estimable collections. Auctions have descriptive themes like Art Deco Design, Fine Art and Antiques, and Jewelry and Fashion so you know when items you're interested in will be up for sale. Books, antiquities, rugs, silver, and Americana are also item categories that hit their auction block. Download their app to be apprised of auctions, follow specific artists, and bid if you can't get to Litchfield.

425 Bantam Rd., Litchfield, 860-567-4661
litchfieldcountyauctions.com

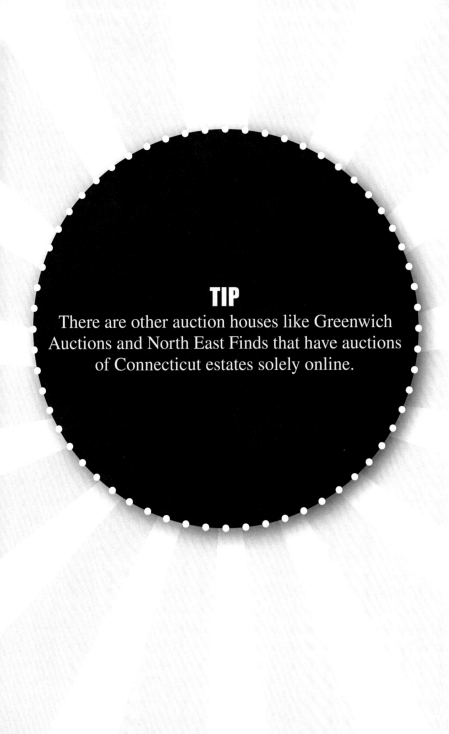

TIP
There are other auction houses like Greenwich Auctions and North East Finds that have auctions of Connecticut estates solely online.

SPEND AN AFTERNOON
AT AN IDEAL THRIFT STORE
AND HELP RESCUED ANIMALS

A thrift store that is organized, well stocked, and cheap; that is housed in a big, historic building with a coffee shop; and that supports animal rescues with the proceeds . . .Well, count me in. PRP R3 stands for Pandemonium Rainforest Project Recycle Reuse Repurpose. There are racks of nice clothing items for four and five dollars each in this 12,000-square-foot former ivory factory, and you can also find lacrosse sticks and items for the house like cute plates and vintage record players. A media area has an eclectic selection of CDs, DVDs, and books that you can crack open to read with your scone and cup of joe. The owner, Allison Sloane, rescues "exotic" animals—birds and reptiles—that often have no place to go when abandoned. She cares for African gray parrots, snakes, cockatiels, and turtles using the proceeds from the thrift store and also presents educational animal programs.

112 W Elm St., Deep River, 860-322-4275
facebook.com/pandemoniumthriftshop

FIND
ONE-OF-A-KIND PIECES
AT THE GUILFORD CRAFT EXPO

Held every year since 1957 on the Guildford Green, the Guilford Craft Expo is a multiday July gathering that draws close to 200 artisans, both local and from across the country. This premier outdoor juried show of American crafts features works for sale in an enormous range of media. Fine art and photography are always well represented, but how about a vibrantly colored handblown glass serving dish or a leather wallet you won't find in stores? Pick up a lemonade and a nosh at one of the food trucks, wander around the tents, and enjoy the live music. There are hands-on activities in the Kids Tent, and craft demonstrations like watching a potter work the wheel add to the art-based experiences. The admission fee funds the Guilford Art Center's educational and community programming.

Guilford Town Green, 31 Whitfield St., Park St. and Broad St., Guilford
203-453-5947, guilfordartcenter.org/expo

STROLL CONNECTICUT'S RODEO DRIVE,
GREENWICH AVENUE

Many Connecticut towns have charming shopping districts on greens with gazebos and white-steepled churches. There's Litchfield and New Milford, Mystic's wonderful West Main Street, and Kent, with shops that curate unusual finds—especially in the home design and women's clothing categories. But for sheer retail volume, variety, and experience, head to New England's version of Rodeo Drive, Greenwich Avenue. A stroll takes you past retailers like Lily Pulitzer and Saks Fifth Avenue as well as home-grown stores such as Hoagland's, the local go-to for elegant gifts; Richard's, a beautiful shop for high-end fashion; and luxury jewelry retailer Betteridge. Two Greenwich brothers started Vineyard Vines, lifestyle brand ASHA by Ashley McCormick is here, and don't overlook the side streets where you'll find local gift store Splurge and women's designer Katie Fong.

Greenwich Ave., from West Putnam Ave. to Railroad Ave., Greenwich
business.greenwichchamber.com/list/ql/shopping-specialty-retail-23#

TIPS

Have a cocktail and appetizer at **The Cottage** or **Happy Monkey**.

Favorite restaurants include **Elm Street Oyster House** and **Orienta**.

People-watch from the patio at **Terra**.

Turn left at Museum Drive and visit the **Bruce Museum**.

The Cottage
49 Greenwich Ave., 203-769-1220
thecottage.kitchen

Happy Monkey
376 Greenwich Ave., 203-405-5787
happymonkeygreenwich.com

Elm Street Oyster House
11 W Elm St., 203-629-5795
elmstreetoysterhouse.com

Orienta
55 Lewis St., 203-489-3394
orientarestaurant.com

Terra
156 Greenwich Ave., 203-629-5222
zhospitalitygroup.com/terra-greenwich/home

Bruce Museum
1 Museum Dr., 203-869-0376
brucemuseum.org

PICK UP
SOMETHING PEWTER
IN WOODBURY

Connecticut was a center of colonial pewter production in the 18th century but other materials took over the housewares market. Luckily, we Nutmeggers cling to tradition. Woodbury Pewter produces items like candlesticks and sconces in a factory with a viewing window and sells their factory seconds at reduced rates on-site. Watch the introductory video and browse the collection of pewter objects made here as well as items from other pewter manufacturers. Take home a reproduction of an early American pewter mug (without the lead that used to be part of the pewter mix), a candy dish, or shell-shaped earrings. Think of this spot for hostess gifts and Father's Day with items like beautifully presented mint julep cups, letter openers, flasks, and money clips. The store also sells non-pewter items like robes, and the company engraves trophies and other items on-site.

860 Main St. S, Woodbury, 203-263-2668
woodburypewter.com

SHOP 'TIL YOU DROP
AT CLINTON PREMIUM OUTLETS

With 70 well-known, brand-name stores selling apparel and footwear for women, men, and children, Clinton Premium Outlets is a destination for everything from back-to-school shopping to searching for special-occasion formal wear. The anchor is Saks Off Fifth, which has women's and men's designer clothes, handbags, and racks of well-priced shoes and boots. Polo Ralph Lauren always has great selections as do the factory stores for J. Crew and Banana Republic. Armani, Calvin Klein, Lucky, Boss, and Michael Kors are on the higher end while Gap, Express, and Levi's are more affordable. If you're a purse lover, peruse the styles at Dooney & Bourke, Kate Spade, Coach, and Vera Bradley. Look for the walkway at what appears to be the end of the stores as you need to cross a parking lot to reach sneaker brands like Nike, New Balance, Puma, and Adidas.

20 Killingworth Tpke., Clinton, 860-664-0700
premiumoutlets.com/outlet/clinton

TIP
Don't come on an empty stomach as there are slim pickings for food.

SEE WHAT NECESSITIES YOU WILL IMPULSIVELY PURCHASE
AT THE BOWERBIRD

With a tagline that reads "Impulsive Necessities," The Bowerbird reveals that they know the psyches of their shoppers. Before you walked in the door you might not have realized that you needed jewelry made with sand from area beaches, a shower curtain with an area nautical map, or a kid's ninja rope. True to its name, there is plenty of bird-themed merchandise like a mallard walking stick, a hummingbird feeder, and a blown-glass oriole with a feather tail. Customers are known to stock up on cards, as there are 60 different greeting card lines represented, many difficult to find elsewhere. In a shopping plaza with plenty of parking, The Bowerbird also carries regionally made food items like Ashlawn Farm Coffee and Bureau's Sugarhouse Maple Kettle Korn.

46 Halls Rd., Old Lyme, 860-434-3562
thebowerbird.com

TIP

The Bowerbird will gift wrap purchases for a small fee and then donate 50 percent to a different local charity every year.

EMBRACE YOUR INNER ARTIST
AT THE RED HOUSE CULTURAL ARTS CENTER

The creative classes offered at the cozy Red House Cultural Arts Center reveal the talents of the local artists who lead workshops, exhibit in the gallery, and sell works in the gift store. Buy theirs or take a class to make your own water-marbled silk scarf or leather macramé bracelet with freshwater pearls, assemble a mosaic clay pendant, or fashion a fused-glass plant stake. Run by a potter and woodworker couple, the space has carried the work of more than 50 local makers. Everything is one of a kind like handmade jewelry, hand-carved wooden oars and bowls, and felt animals. Find unique ceramics like plates, vases, and mugs as well as fine art, soap, candles, and stationery. Look for some of the bestsellers made by the owners: wooden picture frames and ceramic flower frogs and botanicals.

22 Darling Rd., Salem, 860-608-6526
salemredhouse.com

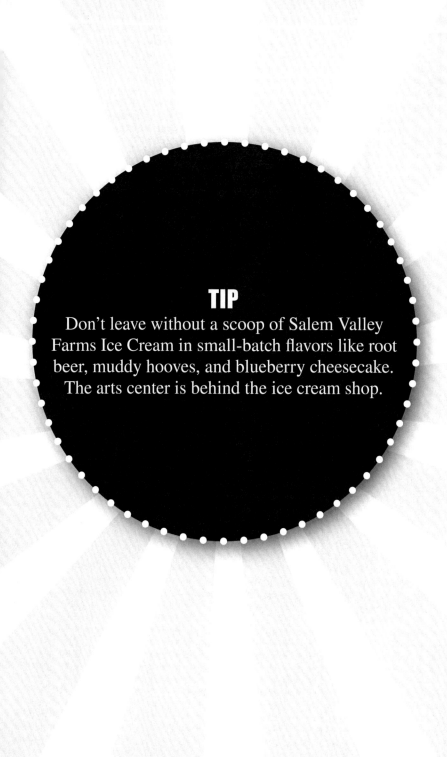

TIP

Don't leave without a scoop of Salem Valley Farms Ice Cream in small-batch flavors like root beer, muddy hooves, and blueberry cheesecake. The arts center is behind the ice cream shop.

GET A JUMP ON YOUR HOLIDAY SHOPPING IN STYLE
AT THE WADSWORTH MANSION

Connecticut knows how to do Christmas: Once December rolls around you will be treated to tree lightings on town greens in places like Bethlehem, "Connecticut's Christmas Town"; visits with Santa; *Messiah* and *Nutcracker* performances; and neighborhoods adorned with lights. Stores are in overdrive as this is their busiest time of the year, so skip the mall and support local shopping events like the Wadsworth Mansion Holiday Bazaar. Formerly the private Long Hill Estate, the Wadsworth Mansion is a stately manor that can be likened to the White House. Kick-start your holiday shopping at this lovely market to find locally produced maple barbeque sauce, tote bags and place mats in cheery prints, jewelry crafted from handblown glass lampwork beads, herbal teas and wellness tonics, and home-baked dog treats. Food and beverages are available on-site to buoy your stamina.

421 Wadsworth St., Middletown, 860-347-1064
wadsworthmansion.com/event-calendar/holiday-bazaar

SUPPORT NONPROFITS
WITH UNIQUE GIFTS
FROM MUSEUM STORES

The state's museums, historical societies, and other nonprofits have shops that are often overlooked as places to find distinctive gifts. Their merchandise comprises items relating to their mission and collections; so, for example, the Mashantucket Pequot Museum & Research Center carries unique items made by Native Americans like handmade wampum and silver and copper jewelry. The large store at the Mark Twain House & Museum obviously has a robust book collection. It also sells a silk scarf printed with the design of a Tiffany stained glass window that was once in the house as well as charms made from vintage typewriter keys set in sterling silver. The small Greenwich Historical Society Museum Store is expertly curated with eye-catching seasonal displays, tasteful silver and porcelain hostess gifts, anchor cuff links, and lovely note cards featuring the American Impressionist paintings on-site. Clever items that tied into a recent sports exhibition curated by the museum included sports bingo and a preppy tote bag emblazoned with pickleball racquets.

47 Strickland Rd., Cos Cob, 203-869-6899
greenwichhistory.org or greenwichhistorymuseumstore.shopsettings.com

Buttonwood Farm in Griswold,
courtesy of the Connecticut Office of Tourism

ACTIVITIES
BY SEASON

SPRING

SUMMER

FALL

Climb through the Treetops at the Adventure Park at Storrs, 71

Take a Fall Foliage Drive in the Quiet Corner, 52

Get into the Halloween Spirit at Plainville's Witch's Dungeon, 130

WINTER

Cross-Country Ski in the Silent Serenity of the Farmington Woods, 72

Dream of Sugar Plum Fairies at *The Nutcracker*, 37

Get a Jump on Your Holiday Shopping in Style at the Wadsworth Mansion, 156

Adventure Park,
courtesy of Anastasia Mills Healy

Hammonasset Beach State Park in Madison,
courtesy of the Connecticut Office of Tourism

SUGGESTED
ITINERARIES

THE CONNECTICUT RIVER VALLEY

ON THE SHORELINE

• •

FAMILY FRIENDLY

GROWN-UP FUN

• •

HARTFORD CULTURE AND HISTORY

Devils Hopyard State Park in East Haddam,
courtesy of the Connecticut Office of Tourism

INDEX

• •

169

Boating in Noank, courtesy of Anastasia Mills Healy